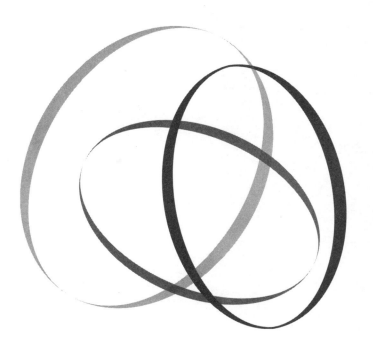

Engage ALL Students
Through Differentiation

By Anne M. Beninghof

**Crystal Springs
BOOKS**

A division of **SDE**™ Staff Development for Educators

Peterborough, New Hampshire

Published by Crystal Springs Books
A division of Staff Development for Educators (SDE)
10 Sharon Road, PO Box 500
Peterborough, NH 03458
1-800-321-0401
www.crystalsprings.com
www.sde.com

Published 2006
Printed in the United States of America
10 09 08 07   2 3 4 5

Library of Congress Cataloging-in-Publication Data

Beninghof, Anne M.
    Engage all students through differentiation / by Anne M. Beninghof.
        p.   cm.
    Includes bibliographical references and index.
    ISBN-13: 978-1-884548-79-6
    ISBN-10: 1-884548-79-2
    1. Lesson planning. 2. Inclusive education. 3. Activity programs in
education. I. Title.
    LB1027.4.B46 2006
    371.3'028--dc22

                                        2006002887

Editor: Sandra J. Taylor
Art Director, Designer, and Production Coordinator: Soosen Dunholter
Book production and illustration: Jill Shaffer

Dedication

For my daughter, Rachel, who allows me to practice many of my teaching ideas on her before taking them into the classroom. She continually encourages and inspires me to be a better teacher.

For the hundreds of teachers around the country who so generously share their ideas with me and with others to improve teaching and learning. Thank you.

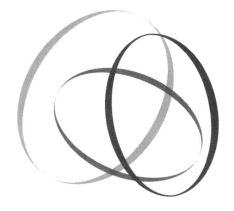

Contents

Strategies for Understanding and Remembering

Strategies for Summarizing

Strategies for Encouraging Participation

Strategies for Review and Practice

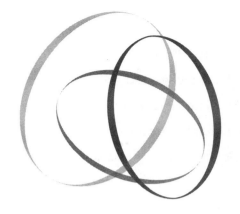

Introduction

The term "differentiation" generates many visions among teachers. Some think immediately of the variety of learning styles of their students. Some think of the wide range of student abilities and skills they see when they teach a new concept. And still others have phrases like *cultural diversity, achievement gap, multiple intelligences,* or *hands-on learning* floating through their minds.

All these visions merge to form the concept of differentiation. Carol Ann Tomlinson, leader in differentiation, describes teachers who differentiate as those who "strive to do whatever it takes to ensure that struggling and advanced learners, students with varied cultural heritages, and children with different background experiences all grow as much as they possibly can each day, each week, and throughout the year." (Tomlinson, 1999, p. 5.) What a challenge this is for teachers!

Why are teachers having to take on a broader challenge of differentiation at this point in time? While there has always been a need to differentiate, there are several current developments in education that are increasing this need. Since the early 1980s, the inclusive education movement has led to pressure on schools to include students with disabilities in general-education classrooms. Research has begun to show significant benefits of inclusive education for all students, and the federal government has reinforced this research with related mandates (IDEA, 1997). As we move into system-wide implementation, we have recognized the need for students with disabilities to go from "presence to progress"—from a basic expectation of being placed in general-education settings to a higher expectation of real academic progress in those settings (Thompson, 2003, p. 6).

Simultaneously, educators have sought ways to help all children achieve high standards of learning. An early emphasis on closing the achievement gap for students of color has morphed into an emphasis on leaving no child behind, no matter what the reason. Again, federal mandates have followed the lead of education professionals. The passage in 2001 of the No Child Left Behind Act imposed new accountability systems on teachers and schools that are meant to promote academic growth even for the most-challenging students.

Finally, the diversity of the population has rapidly changed. Classrooms are filled with children who speak different languages, have varied economic circumstances, grew up with unique cultural experiences, and live in families that don't fit the mold of the 1950s. One glance inside a classroom supports what the U.S. Census Bureau tells us—that our population is becoming much more diverse. Effective teachers recognize the need to provide instruction that matches the individual needs of each of their students.

To help teachers with this challenge, various models for differentiation have been developed. The best models use the growing body of research as an underlying framework but design a process that is user-friendly for classroom teachers. The lesson-planning model proposed in this book accomplishes just that. It combines the aspects of student readiness level and student learning style in a simple-to-follow format. This model has been used successfully across content areas and grade levels, showing its versatility for a wide variety of classroom applications.

Once a lesson-planning structure for differentiation is in place, teachers must decide which instructional strategies will best accomplish the lesson objectives. This book is filled with effective strategies that lend themselves to differentiated instruction. The ideas have been gathered from teachers around the country who are successful at teaching diverse populations of students. Two primary criteria have been used in the selection of these strategies. First, every idea has been teacher-tested. In other words, the strategies have been used in real-life classrooms and have been successful. Second, each idea has been rated "practical" by teachers. The ideas are considered simple enough to be doable—even by today's busy, dedicated teachers. They are also easy to adapt for use in a variety of teaching situations. So, no matter what you are teaching, there are ideas in this book that will help improve your instruction for all students.

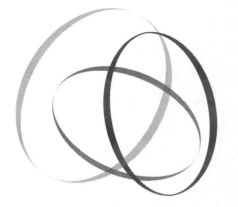

A Lesson Plan Model for Engaging ALL Students

The EAS (Engaging ALL Students) Lesson Plan directly encompasses two principal facets of differentiation—readiness level and learning style. Readiness level refers to a student's entry point when learning a specific piece of content or a particular skill. In any heterogeneous class, teachers will have at least three readiness levels, if not 30! There are likely to be some students who are ready to be challenged with a high level of complexity, such as higher-order thinking, creative application, and a quicker instructional pace. Other students will fall in the middle of the range and will usually have their needs met by the typical content and pacing. Some students in every class will need instruction that is less complex, such as hands-on application, clear directions and steps, and extra time to process the new learning.

The EAS Lesson Plan form provides three distinct spaces for you to write a description of the teaching approach that you will use. The column on the left side is for notations that pertain to the general student body. At the top of the right-hand column is an area for you to describe ways in which the complexity will be ramped up for those students who are ready. Beneath that is an area to list ideas that simplify the complexity so that struggling students will also understand and grasp the instruction. This section of the form allows planning for differentiation based on readiness level. (**Note:** Sometimes in a differentiated lesson, students might be grouped by ability level and be given very different tasks. In this model, most instruction is done as a whole group lesson, with some minor variations offered within that context to accommodate students who need greater or less complexity. Ability grouping can be designed using the EAS format but should be done with caution appropriate to the potential disadvantages of ability grouping [see research by Kulik, 1992].)

Learning style refers to the many conditions under which a student learns best. These include time of day, perceptual modality, seating preferences, lighting, global versus analytic thinking, and much more. Teacher experience and research find that adapting for the learning styles of students can have a significant impact on student achievement. While all the learning-style components have an impact on learning, the research on perceptual modality (the sense used by a person to receive and comprehend information) provides key information on how this impacts the learning of struggling students.

Research on students who are low-achieving, have been identified as having a disability, or are high school dropouts (Dunn, 1988; Dunn & Dunn, 1993; Mohrmann, 1990; Yong & McIntyre, 1992) shows that these students have seven learning-style characteristics in common:

1. Need for frequent movement
2. Need for materials and instruction with a heavy emphasis on visual, kinesthetic, and tactile input
3. Poor auditory perception and memory
4. Preference for receiving instruction later in the day
5. Preference for variety in seating, grouping, and environment
6. Need for an informal classroom design
7. Preference during elementary and middle school years for dim lighting

Because the research shows such strong implications of the impact of learning style for struggling students, especially the need for tactile and kinesthetic input, the EAS Lesson Plan format includes four boxes, one for each of the four perceptual modalities (Visual, Auditory, Kinesthetic, and Tactile). As you are planning your lesson, create opportunities for all perceptual modalities to be addressed. As each modality is integrated into the lesson, check off the corresponding box. The goal for every lesson is to provide ALL students the opportunity to learn through their dominant learning style. The boxes serve as a reminder to review the lesson and ensure that all four modalities are present. As you plan, think "Have I built in a visual (auditory, kinesthetic, tactile) component for my visual (auditory, kinesthetic, tactile) learners?" If the answer is yes, check off the box.

The EAS Lesson Plan works well with all grade levels and all content areas. The following examples will illustrate how to plan for differentiated instruction with a variety of objectives. Embedded in the examples are valuable strategies that are flexible enough to be used with other content objectives, too. And, depending on the age and readiness levels of students, strategies can be adjusted to fit a wide range of learners. Remember that all kids like to have fun while learning (even those middle schoolers), so look for the strategies that you think will motivate and engage your students' brains while also adding fun to the classroom. Variations and tips are provided at the end of each strategy description to help you tweak ideas to work best for you.

EAS Lesson Plan

Instructional Objective _____

V   A   K   T

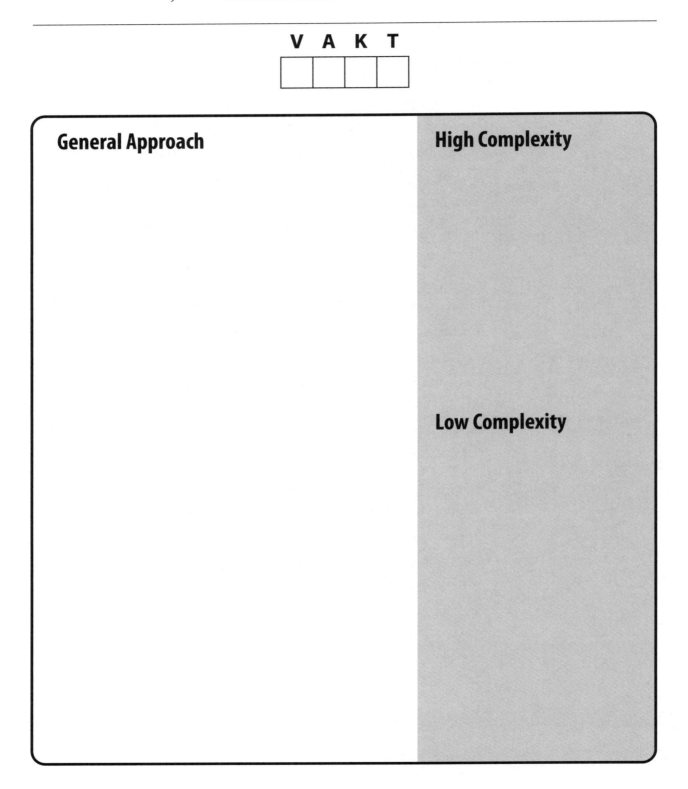

General Approach

High Complexity

Low Complexity

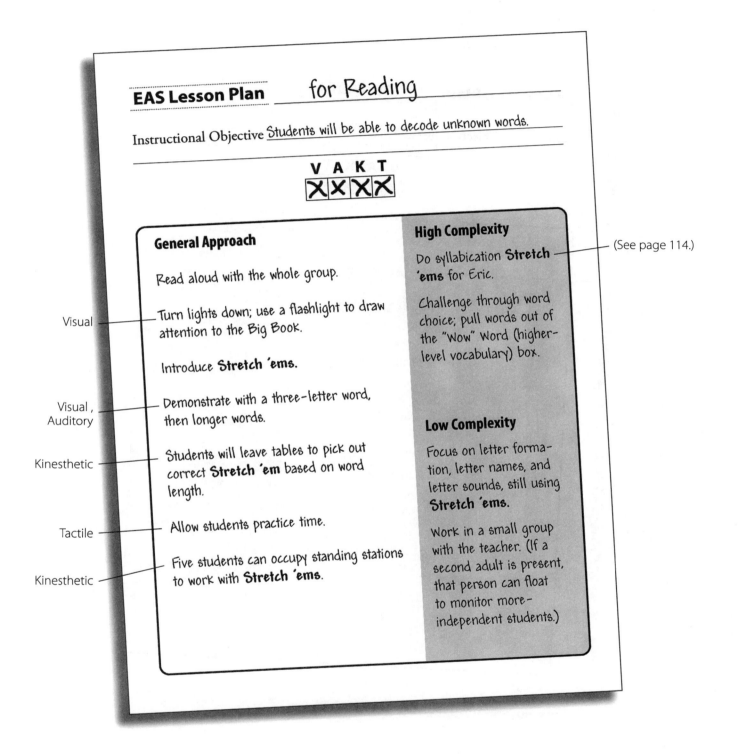

EAS Lesson Plan — for Reading

Instructional Objective <u>Students will be able to decode unknown words.</u>

V A K T
[X][X][X][X]

General Approach

Read aloud with the whole group.

Visual — Turn lights down; use a flashlight to draw attention to the Big Book.

Introduce **Stretch 'ems.**

Visual, Auditory — Demonstrate with a three-letter word, then longer words.

Kinesthetic — Students will leave tables to pick out correct **Stretch 'em** based on word length.

Tactile — Allow students practice time.

Kinesthetic — Five students can occupy standing stations to work with **Stretch 'ems.**

High Complexity

Do syllabication **Stretch 'ems** for Eric. — (See page 114.)

Challenge through word choice; pull words out of the "Wow" Word (higher-level vocabulary) box.

Low Complexity

Focus on letter formation, letter names, and letter sounds, still using **Stretch 'ems.**

Work in a small group with the teacher. (If a second adult is present, that person can float to monitor more-independent students.)

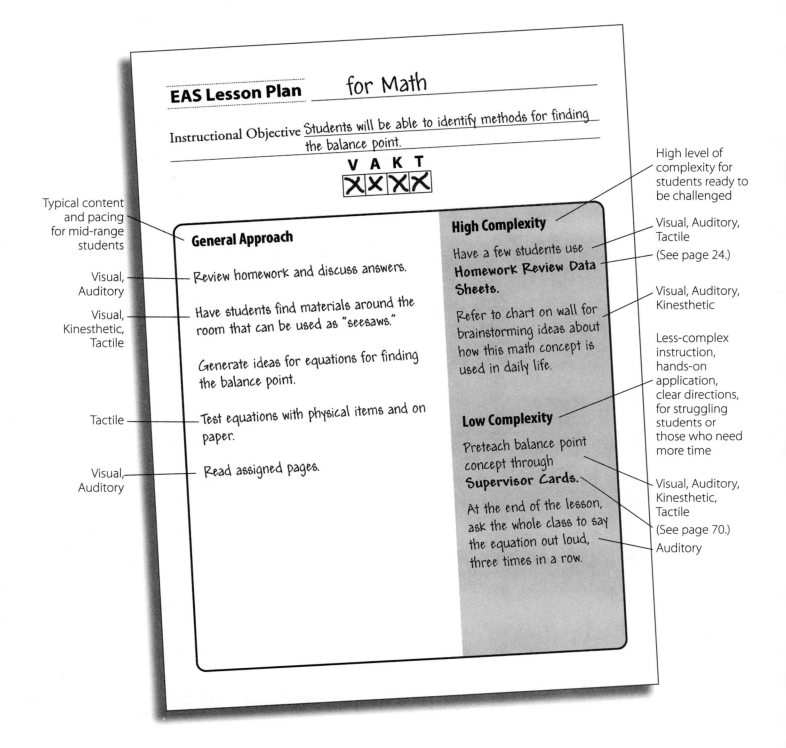

EAS Lesson Plan _____for Math_____

Instructional Objective <u>Students will be able to identify methods for finding</u>
<u>the balance point.</u>

V A K T
☒☒☒

Typical content and pacing for mid-range students

Visual, Auditory

Visual, Kinesthetic, Tactile

Tactile

Visual, Auditory

General Approach

- Review homework and discuss answers.

- Have students find materials around the room that can be used as "seesaws."

- Generate ideas for equations for finding the balance point.

- Test equations with physical items and on paper.

- Read assigned pages.

High level of complexity for students ready to be challenged

Visual, Auditory, Tactile
(See page 24.)

Visual, Auditory, Kinesthetic

Less-complex instruction, hands-on application, clear directions, for struggling students or those who need more time

Visual, Auditory, Kinesthetic, Tactile
(See page 70.)

Auditory

High Complexity

Have a few students use **Homework Review Data Sheets.**

Refer to chart on wall for brainstorming ideas about how this math concept is used in daily life.

Low Complexity

Preteach balance point concept through **Supervisor Cards.**

At the end of the lesson, ask the whole class to say the equation out loud, three times in a row.

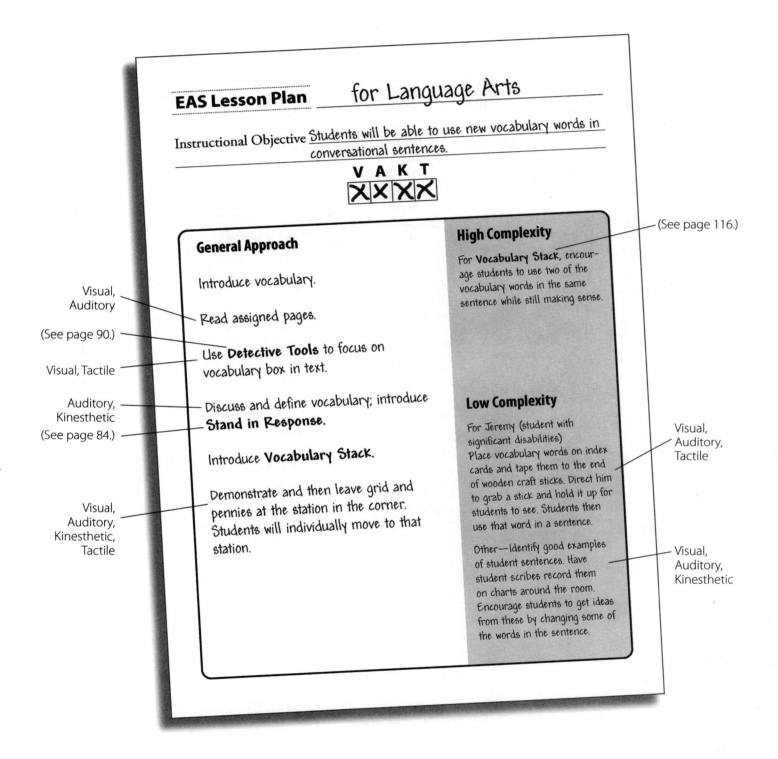

EAS Lesson Plan for Language Arts

Instructional Objective Students will be able to use new vocabulary words in conversational sentences.

V A K T
X X X X

General Approach

Introduce vocabulary.

Read assigned pages.

Use **Detective Tools** to focus on vocabulary box in text.

Discuss and define vocabulary; introduce **Stand in Response.**

Introduce **Vocabulary Stack.**

Demonstrate and then leave grid and pennies at the station in the corner. Students will individually move to that station.

Visual, Auditory

(See page 90.)

Visual, Tactile

Auditory, Kinesthetic
(See page 84.)

Visual, Auditory, Kinesthetic, Tactile

High Complexity

For **Vocabulary Stack**, encourage students to use two of the vocabulary words in the same sentence while still making sense.

(See page 116.)

Low Complexity

For Jeremy (student with significant disabilities) Place vocabulary words on index cards and tape them to the end of wooden craft sticks. Direct him to grab a stick and hold it up for students to see. Students then use that word in a sentence.

Visual, Auditory, Tactile

Other—Identify good examples of student sentences. Have student scribes record them on charts around the room. Encourage students to get ideas from these by changing some of the words in the sentence.

Visual, Auditory, Kinesthetic

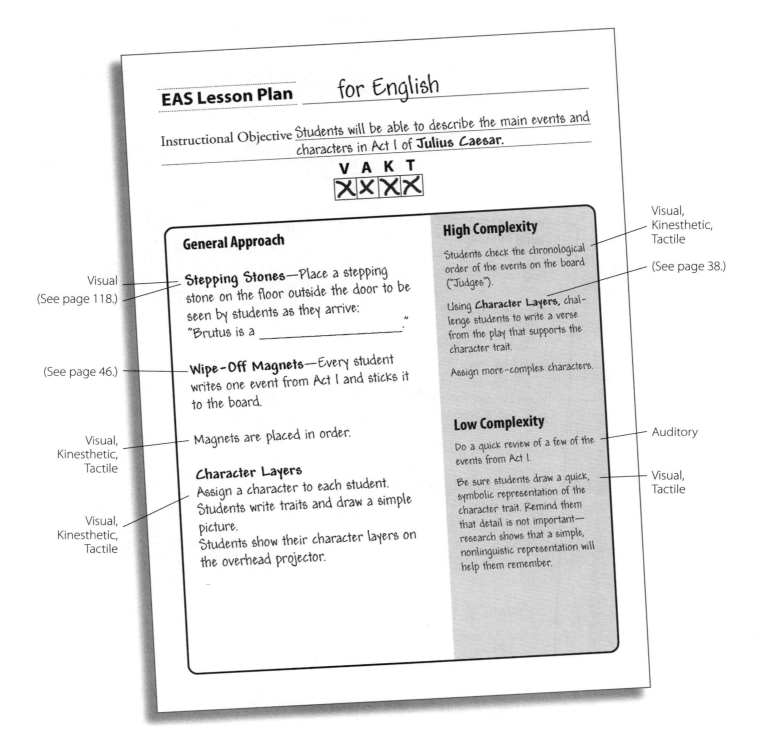

EAS Lesson Plan   for English

Instructional Objective Students will be able to describe the main events and characters in Act I of **Julius Caesar.**

V A K T
X X X X

General Approach

Visual
(See page 118.)

Stepping Stones—Place a stepping stone on the floor outside the door to be seen by students as they arrive: "Brutus is a _____."

(See page 46.)

Wipe-Off Magnets—Every student writes one event from Act I and sticks it to the board.

Visual, Kinesthetic, Tactile

Magnets are placed in order.

Visual, Kinesthetic, Tactile

Character Layers
Assign a character to each student. Students write traits and draw a simple picture.
Students show their character layers on the overhead projector.

High Complexity

Visual, Kinesthetic, Tactile

Students check the chronological order of the events on the board ("Judges").

(See page 38.)

Using **Character Layers**, challenge students to write a verse from the play that supports the character trait.

Assign more-complex characters.

Low Complexity

Auditory

Do a quick review of a few of the events from Act I.

Visual, Tactile

Be sure students draw a quick, symbolic representation of the character trait. Remind them that detail is not important—research shows that a simple, nonlinguistic representation will help them remember.

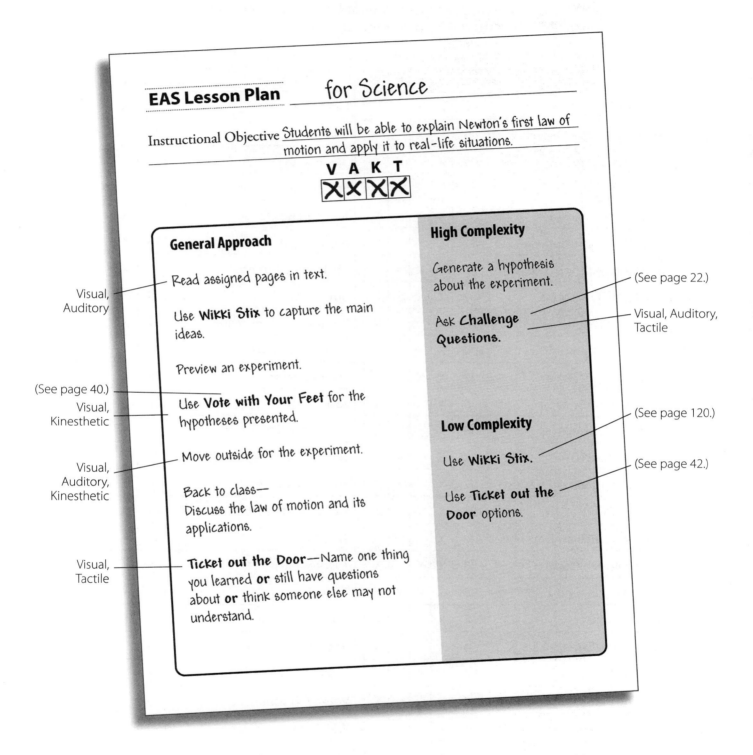

EAS Lesson Plan _for Science_

Instructional Objective _Students will be able to explain Newton's first law of motion and apply it to real-life situations._

V A K T
[X][X][ ][X]

General Approach

Visual, Auditory → Read assigned pages in text.

Use **Wikki Stix** to capture the main ideas.

Preview an experiment.

(See page 40.)
Visual, Kinesthetic → Use **Vote with Your Feet** for the hypotheses presented.

Visual, Auditory, Kinesthetic → Move outside for the experiment.

Back to class—
Discuss the law of motion and its applications.

Visual, Tactile → **Ticket out the Door**—Name one thing you learned **or** still have questions about **or** think someone else may not understand.

High Complexity

Generate a hypothesis about the experiment. → (See page 22.)

Ask **Challenge Questions**. → Visual, Auditory, Tactile

Low Complexity

Use **Wikki Stix**. → (See page 120.)

Use **Ticket out the Door** options. → (See page 42.)

Strategies and Perceptual Modalities Table

Almost everything that happens in a classroom has a visual and auditory component to it. For the purposes of this table, the dominant modalities of a strategy are marked.

STRATEGY	PAGE NO.	V	A	K	T
4 x 6 Posters	60	X	X		X
Alternate Text Vocabulary	48		X		
Board Relay	108	X		X	X
Boomerang Bookmarks	54	X			X
Brain Bags	102	X			X
Bubble-Wrap Response	82		X		X
Challenge Authority Cards	28		X		
Challenge Questions	22		X		
Character Layers	38	X		X	X
Colorful Speech	104	X			X
Cup Stacking	92	X	X	X	X
Detective Tools	90	X			X
Find the Balance	36	X		X	X
Glove Balloons	62	X		X	X
Graphic Organizer Puzzles	52	X		X	X
Group Graffiti	58	X	X		X
Homework Review Data Sheet	24	X			X
Lightbulb Moments	88	X	X		X
Make a Connection	56		X	X	X
Memory Makers	68	X			X
Millionaire Game	64	X		X	X
Participation Punch	80		X		X
Pass the Plate	110	X			X
Pattern Towers	94	X			X
Personal Meter	34	X			X

STRATEGY	PAGE NO.	V	A	K	T
Pick a Path	30	X			X
Shrink It	74	X			X
Spelling Bells	106		X		X
Spelling Keyboard	98	X	X		X
Stand in Response	84	X		X	
Stepping Stones	118	X	X	X	
Sticky-Dot Editing	32	X			X
Stretch 'ems	114	X	X		X
Subtraction Summary	72	X	X		
Supervisor Cards	70	X	X		
Sweet Sheets	78	X			
Task Cards	26				X
Tennis Spelling	100	X		X	X
Text Message Summary	76	X			X
Text Retell Cards	50		X	X	
Ticket out the Door	42	X			X
Tie a Knot	44	X	X	X	X
T-Notes Plus	66	X			X
TP the Room	112	X		X	X
Twist and Spell	96	X			X
Vocabulary Stack	116	X	X		X
Voice Bells	86	X	X		X
Vote with Your Feet	40	X		X	
Wikki Stix	120	X			X
Wipe-Off Magnets	46	X		X	X

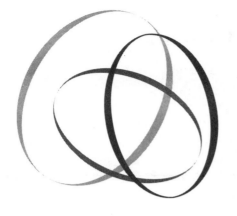

Putting the Strategies to Work

Now that you have had some experience with the EAS Lesson Plan format, it is time for the strategies! The following ideas can be included in many of the EAS lessons you will plan. Keep in mind the instructional standards for your classroom as you browse through the ideas, and be sure to dog-ear the pages that are a clear fit. Then, sit with a colleague or grade-level team and discuss some of the other strategies. Working together, you will be able to create methods for tweaking the strategies to develop even more ideas!

Remember that each strategy can be adapted to use with a broad grade range—or readiness level. While the ideas have been marked with a suggested grade range, some students may need instructional interventions from a lower or higher level than their current grade. One of my goals, as a teacher trainer and author, is to help teachers understand that older students need interactive, engaging strategies just as much as younger students do. I use all kinds of "elementary" strategies in middle school and high school, and they work beautifully! As I speak with teachers all around the country, they get excited by this approach to teaching and repeatedly e-mail me about the value of using these ideas with older students. I hope you have the same positive experience, no matter what level you teach.

Challenge Questions (3–8)

All students benefit from engaging in discussion that includes higher-order thinking. It is the teacher's responsibility to ask questions and assign tasks that stimulate this kind of thinking, without getting bogged down in too much auditory input. Challenge Questions provide teachers and students with readily available questions and tasks, incorporating a tactile medium, so that all students will be interested and engaged.

Materials

Challenge Questions (see reproducibles, pages 124–127)
Small bag or paper sack

How To

1. Make a single copy of the Challenge Questions most related to your curriculum.
2. Cut the paper so that each question is separated, and place the questions in a small bag.
3. At an appropriate point in the lesson, hand the bag to a student and direct him to pull out a question and read it aloud.
4. Ask students for responses.
5. Return the question to the bag for future use.

Variations

- Have students generate Challenge Questions to add to the bag.
- When you see a need to add some spice or challenge to your lecture, pull out a question yourself.

- If students are working in small groups, such as literature circles, provide each group with a Challenge Questions bag to keep their discussions moving along at a higher level.

- Instead of placing questions into a bag, tape them onto objects such as wooden craft sticks or ping pong balls, or put them inside balloons. This will add an additional tactile component to the strategy.

- Place each question in a separate envelope and leave the envelopes unsealed. Draw a large question mark on the outside of the envelope. Post the envelopes around the room. When in need of a higher-level question, ask a student to get out of her seat, pick an envelope, and read the question inside. This gives a kinesthetic learner some opportunity for movement.

Tip

☆ Challenge Questions can be handed to students as a single sheet of paper; however, cutting them into strips and placing them into a bag adds some spice. Students are more intrigued because of the randomness of choice and the tactile interaction.

Pick a person who is currently famous. How does this science concept relate to his ___ er life?

How might your mother (father, grandp____nt) apply this science ___ept to her life?

Does this science concept remind you of any othe____ studied this year? H____

What rhyme or rap can you develop to help someone remember this science concept?

If you were teaching this science concept to someone, how would you teach i____ ___t way?

If you were writing a fictional story that involved this science concept, what would the title of the story be?

Homework Review Data Sheet (4–8)

Homework review can be a challenging time for struggling *and* gifted students. The struggling students may need a lengthy, in-depth review of each of the homework problems to fully grasp the skill or content. While this is taking place, the gifted students may become bored and tune out. Homework Review Data Sheets can provide more-able students a higher-level task that is still connected to the content being discussed.

Materials

Homework Review Data Sheet (see reproducible, page 128)

How To

1. Make several copies of the data sheet, and if desired, laminate them so they can be reused.
2. Choose one type of data you would like collected and check it off at the top of the page.
3. Distribute the data sheets to students who have mastered the content being reviewed and ask them to collect the data as described on their sheet.
4. Review the data and share your conclusions with the class. Reflect on the data and adjust your instruction as appropriate.

Variations

- Change the type of data prompts at the top of the data sheet to more closely reflect your content area. For example, in math, one of the prompts might be "The number of times addition, subtraction, multiplication, or division was used." In language arts, a data prompt might be "The number of answers given in full sentences."

- Ask the students to generate ideas for the type of data that might be helpful to collect. Ask them to support their ideas with strong reasoning.

- Share the original data with the class and ask them to interpret it. Discuss ideas for changing the outcomes.

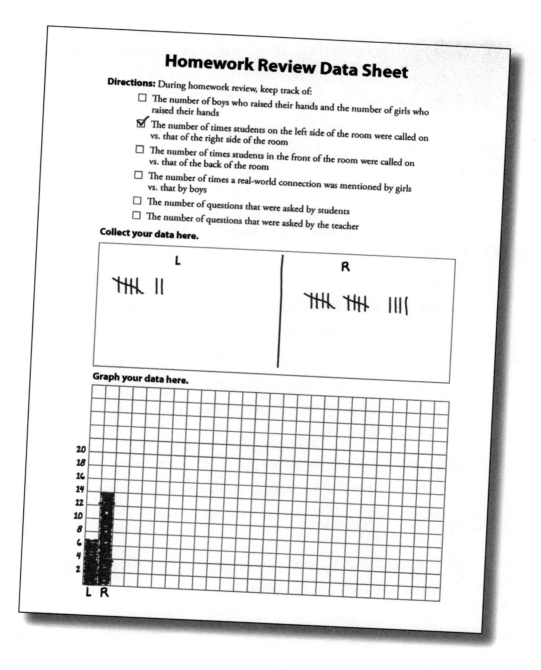

Task Cards (1–8)

In a heterogeneous class, there are usually a few students who grasp the material quickly and are finished before others. Left to their own devices, they can become bored, serve as a distraction to others, or engage in off-task behaviors. Task Cards are a tool for involving these students in complementary material until the rest of the class is ready to move forward.

Materials

Task Cards (see reproducibles, pages 129-133)

How To

1. Make copies of the Task Cards that are most suited to the level of your students. If desired, laminate them for durability and reuse.

2. Explain to students that there are certain tasks that they must do first. You will decide, based on each student, what tasks to require in order to have evidence of their understanding and mastery. The required tasks will be written on the top of the card.

3. When a student has finished the "First" or "Must Do" tasks, he can choose one (or more) of the tasks from the bottom of the card. These are creative, higher-level-thinking tasks that can be applied to any content within that curricular domain.

4. Decide whether you want the students to show you their completed work. Usually, these tasks are meant to be independent work and not be completed for a grade.

Variations

- Make your own Task Cards in different content areas. Leave space at the top to generate the "First" or "Must Do" tasks. The choices on the lower portion of the card should meet four criteria: They should be fun, creative, a higher level of thinking, and generic enough to fit different lesson content. This last criterion is a huge time-saver for the teacher!

- Proclaim one day each month as "Free Day" and allow all students to work on the tasks on the lower part of the card. This will provide all students, even those workers who do not finish quickly, with access to the cards' activities.

Tips

☆ Store the cards in a place where students can easily access them when they have finished their work.

☆ Some of the tasks may require more time than students have in one period. Provide a place for students to store any unfinished tasks until they can complete them.

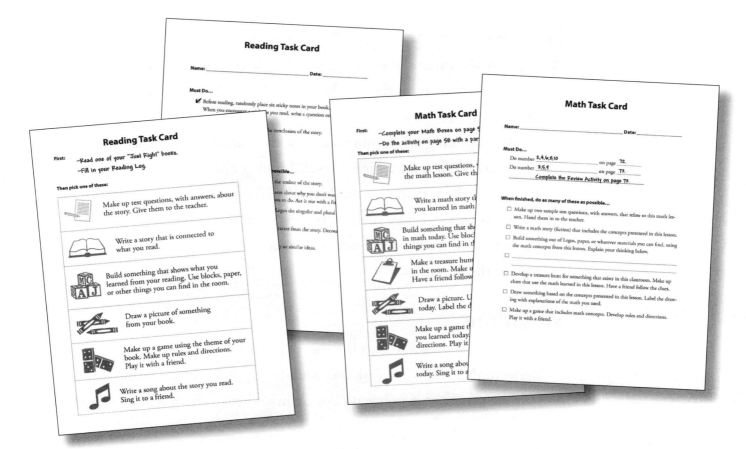

Challenge Authority Cards (4–8)

Higher-level thinking involves the ability to examine material critically and question its validity. By encouraging students to challenge authority in structured ways, we are developing strong thinkers. The Challenge Authority Cards provide this structure and encouragement and can be used on the spot with almost any curriculum.

Materials

Challenge Authority Cards (see reproducible, page 134)
Construction paper or card stock

How To

1. Separate the cards and back them with a piece of construction paper or card stock to increase the durability and life of the cards (or simply laminate them).

2. At the beginning of a lesson, choose a few students in the class who are ready to benefit from a higher-level-thinking task. Hand them each a card. Explain to them that they will be multitasking—paying attention to the lesson while also doing the task described on the card.

3. Call on these students to respond to their task at the appropriate time during the lesson.

Variations

● Encourage students to don the role of a known authority figure as they perform their task. For example, a student might pretend to be the principal, the president, a police officer, or an authority figure from a movie. By playing a role, students may be more comfortable challenging the teacher or other educational experts.

- Challenge Authority Cards can be used as part of a whole-group discussion. Put the cards inside an envelope and have a student remove one. Challenge all the students to do the task described. Enhance the activity with a discussion on the advantages and disadvantages of challenging authority, as well as the best ways to present these challenges.

- Make your own Challenge Authority Cards by writing your own content, based on the lessons you will be including. For example, in a social studies class, a card might suggest that a student look for propaganda or examples of governmental mishandling of an event.

Tip

☆ Before using this strategy, be sure that you are comfortable with students challenging your points of view. While it is healthy to foster this type of critical thinking, it will backfire if it causes you to become defensive or upset with the student.

Listen for a point that the teacher makes that you think you could debate. Debate the teacher, using supportive examples or evidence to prove your point.

Prepare a false answer to one of the questions, and try to convince the teacher or students that you are correct.

Question the text. Did the textbook authors make any errors? Use any poor examples? Have a biased perspective? Leave out something essential?

Look for cultural bias in the lesson. Would other cultures view it the same way? Make the same choices? Disagree?

How could you "fix" this experiment/game/situation (i.e., cheat) so that the outcome would be different?

Pick a Path (2–8)

Effective problem solvers know several different ways to approach a problem. If one approach doesn't seem to be working, they can flexibly shift to another method. Pick a Path is an instructional technique that helps students become aware of their problem-solving patterns and encourages them to broaden their approaches to various activities in school.

Materials

Pick a Path (see reproducible, page 135) for each student

Water-based, wipe-off marker for each student

How To

1. Make copies of the reproducible, laminate for repeated use, and distribute to the students.

2. Instruct the students to list the various approaches to problem-solving in each of the pathways. For example, in math, a student might write "addi-tion," "subtraction," "multiplication," "division," and "other."

3. As students respond to problems, have them make an X on the path they used. For example, let's say you gave them the following word problem:

    "Sara, Eboni, and Kayla were playing together. Sara's mother brought out a plate with 9 cookies. If the girls each get the same amount, how many cookies will each girl have?"

    Some students might quickly use division to solve the problem, while others might use addition.

4. Ask the students to review the paths over time to determine if they tend to underuse or overuse any paths. Discuss the benefits of using different paths and the need to be flexible problem solvers.

Variations

- Use Pick a Path for tracking the genres of reading that students are choosing during free-choice times.

- If you notice that students have a tendency to overuse a certain approach to writing, for example "first, second, third," or "in conclusion," design a Pick a Path that will aid them in recording and reflecting on this data.

- Design Pick a Path forms that have more or fewer paths, depending on the need.

- Allow students to decorate their own pathways, adding words or pictures that reflect their feelings along the way.

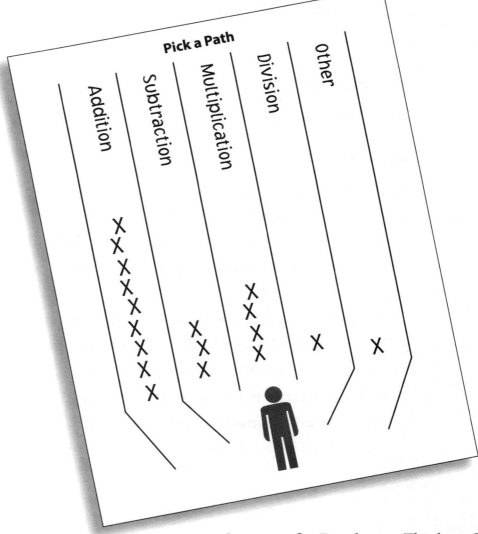

Sticky-Dot Editing (2–8)

Peer editing, a process through which students provide each other with feedback on their writing, has several benefits. It provides students with practice in accepting feedback. It shows students how to think like a reader as well as a writer. And it encourages students to explore different perspectives. Sometimes, however, students are hesitant to provide critical feedback to each other or to consider suggested changes. Sticky-Dot Editing is a strategy that structures the feedback and correction process so that students can experience all the benefits.

Materials

Reusable adhesive dots in two colors

How To

1. Provide each student with two dots of each color.
2. Assign each color a meaning. For example:
   - Color # 1 = "Great," "Well done," or "I really liked this part."
   - Color # 2 = "Consider changing this," "Confusing," or "Could be better."
3. Direct the students to partner with another student.
4. Explain that students are to read their partner's writing assignment and place all four dots on the work. Two dots should be placed as positive feedback, and two dots as constructive feedback.
5. When the students have finished reading and Sticky-Dot Editing, have them explain to their partners their reasons for placing the dots as they did.

6. The original author of the paper then decides what changes, if any, to make, leaving the dots in place on the paper.

7. Sit with each student to conference about his or her writing. Ask the author to explain the feedback represented by the dots and discuss the rationale for making (or not making) changes.

8. Collect the reusable dots for future use.

Variations

● For younger students, one dot of each color may be enough. For older students with longer pieces of writing, more dots may be appropriate.

● Students can use Sticky-Dot Editing to edit their own work, too. This may be a good start for writers who are extremely shy or uncomfortable sharing their work.

Tips

☆ Place sticky dots on a plastic or laminated surface when finished. Store the dots in an envelope for easy access during the next peer-editing session.

☆ Avoid using red dots. Red, in schools, is usually associated with "wrong." Students will be more comfortable providing and receiving feedback if it is viewed as helpful, rather than as strongly critical.

☆ If only white dots are available, have students use a colored marker or crayon to color the dots.

Personal Meter (1–5)

One of the goals most teachers share is to develop independent thinkers. Yet in group settings, it can be difficult for students to feel comfortable voicing their own opinions. Peer influence is very strong. A Personal Meter is a tool for encouraging students to form independent opinions on a variety of topics.

Materials

Personal Meter (see reproducible, page 136) for each student

Brads

How To

1. Make copies of the reproducible, cut out the half-circle shapes and the arrows, and laminate them.

2. Attach one arrow to each meter with a brad inserted at the dot.

3. Give the students each a meter and direct them to place it on their desks, with the straight side at the bottom.

4. Choose the words you would like students to write on their Personal Meters. For example, one end might have "Strongly Agree" and the other "Strongly Disagree." Older students might use "Pro" and "Con."

5. Pose a statement to which students should respond. For example, "Your brain is affected by what you eat."

6. Model for students how to move the arrow to point to the place on the meter that best represents their opinion on the statement.

7. Have students hold up their meters. Allow students to scan the room to see other opinions. Guide a discussion about the differences and similarities.

8. Continue with other statements as appropriate to the content.

Variations

- Personal Meters can be used to communicate a variety of things. Frustration levels can be noted by writing "I understand it!" on one end and "I'm very frustrated!" on the other.
- Work quality can be self-assessed on the meters. Mark the meters from 1 to 10. Have students use the meters to indicate their perspective on the quality of their work.

Tips

- ☆ Place a bit of sticky tack on the back of each meter so it will stay in place on the corner of the desk.
- ☆ Be sure to use your own meter throughout the day as a model for your students. If using a frustration meter, let them see that adults get frustrated, too, and then model solutions for dealing with frustration. If using a meter to assess quality, purposefully model a piece of your own work that is of lesser quality and then show your corrections and improvements.

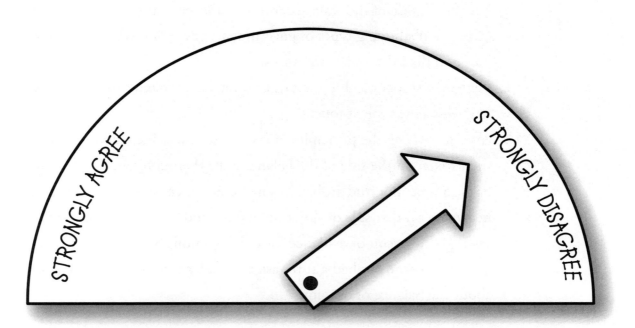

Find the Balance (2–8)

To develop thoughtful opinions and make good decisions, students must be able to weigh options and their outcomes. Find the Balance is a strategy designed to allow students a visual and tactile method for weighing opposing ideas or views and basing their decisions on the results.

Materials

A two-sided balance scale

Chips, pennies, or other small tokens

How To

1. Label each side of the scale according to the two ideas being compared. For example, if studying types of government, one side might represent democracy and the other side communism.

2. Give each student a chip, penny, or other small token. All students must have the same type of token.

3. After discussing the principles of each idea, direct the students to place their token on the side of the balance scale that represents their opinion. For example, if a student believes in a tenet of communism, she can place her token on that side of the scale. As the students place their tokens, they must give a reason or evidence for their opinion.

4. When everyone has had a turn, ask the students to make observations about the balance of opinions.

Variation

● Combine this activity with a math lesson on finding the balance point. Ask students to think of ways to change the balance.

Tips

☆ If a two-sided balance scale is not available, you can make a balance by using an object, such as a soft drink can, for the fulcrum, and resting a yardstick across it.

☆ When using a yardstick and can, be prepared for the tokens to fall off if one side becomes much heavier than the other. Use this moment as a chance to recognize the "winning" opinion.

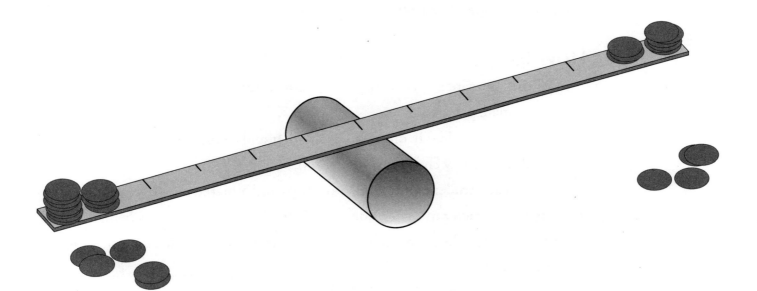

Character Layers (5–8)

As students progress through the grades, they increasingly encounter characters in texts that are complex. This is true in fictional works, as well as in historical and contemporary writings. Character Layers is an instructional strategy that helps students recognize the various traits of an individual and how those traits may build upon or conflict with each other.

Materials

Leftover scraps of laminate or clear-plastic page protectors (available where office supplies are sold)

Water-based, wipe-off markers

How To

1. Cut the laminate or plastic page protectors into strips, each measuring approximately 2 x 6 inches.
2. Stack six strips directly on top of each other and staple them together at one of the narrow ends (see illustration).
3. Provide each student with one set of strips and a marker.
4. Assign a character to each student. If there are several characters being studied, assign the more complicated characters to the students most ready for a challenge.
5. Direct the students to write their character's name on the first strip. On each successive strip, have them write a character trait of that individual and draw a simple, symbolic representation of that trait. For example, if studying Brutus from Shakespeare's *Julius Caesar,* a student might write the word "murderous" and draw a dagger. On the next strip, the student might

write "confused" and draw a simple face with that expression. The words and drawings should progress from left to right (see illustration) and not overlap each other.

6. After students have created their character layers, select one student at a time to show his layers on the overhead projector.

Variations

- Use the strips to show a process with steps that build upon each other. For example, show the steps in photosynthesis or the layers of the earth.
- Use the strips to demonstrate the correct order of the food chain or any other hierarchy.
- Make larger ones for teaching students about multiple line graphs. Students draw a different line on each layer and then see how they overlay each other.

Tip

☆ For easy cleanup, just hold the strips under running water for a few seconds and shake them dry.

Vote with Your Feet (2–8)

Ongoing assessment is a necessary part of effective instruction. Vote with Your Feet utilizes a kinesthetic response to give teachers some quick assessment information. It also provides students with a chance to share opinions and connect more personally to the content.

Materials

Voting signs (see reproducibles, pages 137-138)

How To

1. Make a copy of both voting signs.
2. Post the "Strongly Disagree" sign on the far left side of the front wall of the classroom and the "Strongly Agree" sign on the far right side of the front wall.
3. Instruct students on the concept of a continuum—from strongly disagree to strongly agree, with many intermediate positions.
4. At an appropriate time during the lesson, ask students to express their opinion by voting with their feet. Explain that you will read a statement to them. They are to stand along an imaginary continuum in the front of the room, based on their opinion of the statement. For example, during a science lesson that includes a hypothesis, students might vote on whether the hypothesis will be proven. Other examples include:
   - opinion statements on political or social issues, such as "Children watch too much television"
   - confidence probes, such as "I feel ready to take the quiz"

- content knowledge true/false statements, such as "The square root of 25 is 5"

5. Direct the students to move quickly into position. Ask them to notice where classmates are standing.

6. If time permits, ask a few students to explain why they voted as they did.

Tip

☆ Once the voting signs are posted, leave them up for the rest of the year. Then you can use the Vote with Your Feet strategy at any moment, without any additional preparation.

Ticket out the Door (3–8)

Just as students vary in ability levels, they also vary in what motivates them to be engaged. Some will find the teacher's smile and attention motivation enough, while others need a little extra incentive to stay focused. The Ticket out the Door strategy offers some additional motivation for students and also affords the teacher feedback on the learning that has taken place.

Materials

Ticket out the Door (see reproducible, page 139)

How To

1. Make copies of the reproducible and cut up the tickets.
2. Distribute a ticket to each student at the beginning of the lesson. Explain that they will be expected to sign and hand in their tickets in order to leave class at the end of the period (or to go to lunch, recess, etc.). If they do not have a completed ticket, they will not be excused.
3. On the board or overhead, list the three options that students can write on their tickets:
   - something they learned in the lesson
   - a question they have about the lesson
   - a question they think someone else might have about the lesson (the most important option to offer struggling students, as it reduces the risk of embarrassment and increases the likelihood of honesty)
4. Explain the three options on the board and give appropriate examples.
5. Shortly before the end of the lesson time, remind students to fill out their tickets.

As students are preparing to leave the room, stand at the door and collect the tickets. Review the student responses to make instructional decisions about the need for re-teaching and next steps.

Variations

- Secondary students may be more motivated by authentic raffle tickets (available at office supply stores) or scraps of paper.
- Place tickets in a container and pull a few at random for simple rewards such as bonus points or a free homework pass.

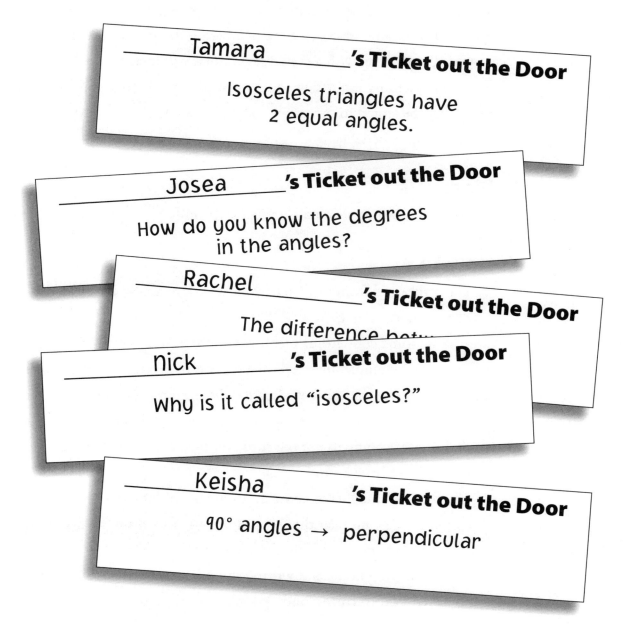

_____Tamara_____'s Ticket out the Door

Isosceles triangles have
2 equal angles.

_____Josea_____'s Ticket out the Door

How do you know the degrees
in the angles?

_____Rachel_____'s Ticket out the Door

The difference bet...

_____Nick_____'s Ticket out the Door

Why is it called "isosceles?"

_____Keisha_____'s Ticket out the Door

90° angles → perpendicular

Tie a Knot   (K–8)

One of our culture's age-old memory tricks is to "tie a string around your finger." This quaint approach to remembering things is based on the idea that a physical act, along with a concrete product, will increase the likelihood of retention. Memory experts agree! Using multiple memory paths makes it more likely that the stored information will be accessed. The Tie a Knot strategy taps into these same benefits.

Materials

Piece of thick cord, approximately 6 feet in length

How To

1. Hang the cord from the top of your white (or chalk) board so that it dangles down freely.

2. Choose some content for memorization that has a small, discreet list of items. For example, five steps in a process or seven days of the week.

3. After teaching the content, describe the notion of "tie a string around your finger" to aid in remembering important things. Explain to the students that they are going to use the cord and the board to remember the important points of the lesson.

4. Choose two students to come up to the board. Direct one student to tie a knot in the cord near the top and the other to write the first point to be remembered next to the knot (see illustration).

5. Continue tying knots and writing the subsequent points until all the items are listed next to corresponding knots.

6. Have the class review the items, first out loud, then silently, and then with their eyes closed.

7. Erase the board, but leave the knots in place. Ask the students to open their eyes and silently recall the items that were next to the knots. After silent reflection, call on individual students to label each knot.

Variations

- Give each student a piece of thin cord, approximately 12 inches long. As you review the items on the board, direct students to tie their own knots on their cords.

- Have cords of different colors available. When trying to memorize characteristics of different items, hang different-colored cords. For example, if studying the characteristics of editing and revising simultaneously, a gold cord could represent editing and a blue cord revising.

Tips

☆ Tape smaller cords onto the side of the students' desks so that they are available to them at all times.

☆ Choose the most kinesthetic or tactile students to come to the board and tie the knots.

☆ Suggest that students use this strategy at home when they are trying to memorize information for a test.

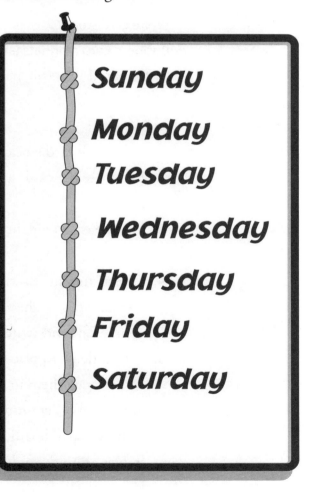

Wipe-Off Magnets (K–8)

Activities that get students up out of their seats also get blood flowing to their brains. Experiencing kinesthetic and tactile input also allows some students to comprehend and retain information at a higher level. Wipe-Off Magnets provide a simple way to accomplish both of these outcomes.

Materials

White card stock

Business-card magnets (available where office supplies are sold)

Water-based, wipe-off markers

How To

1. Cut white card stock to business-card size.

2. Laminate the cards and adhere them to the magnets, creating Wipe-Off Magnets.

3. Provide each student with a Wipe-Off Magnet and a water-based, wipe-off marker.

4. Direct students to write information on their magnets relevant to the class. For example, at the end of Act I of *Julius Caesar*, ask each student to think of an event and write it on the magnet.

5. Ask students to place their magnets on the board at the front of the room and arrange them in correct chronological sequence, in alphabetical or numerical order, into categories, etc. (If you do not have a magnetic white-board or chalkboard, consider using the side of a filing cabinet, the metal frames around windows and doors, or whatever is magnetic in your room. Be creative!)

6. When the lesson is finished, ask students to wipe off the magnets with a damp paper towel and return them to your desk.

Variation

- Wipe-Off Magnets can be used to sort all kinds of information. Here are just a few ideas:
    - ~Words into parts-of-speech categories
    - ~Numbers into even and odd groups
    - ~Months in chronological order
    - ~Countries into hemispheres
    - ~Foods into food groups
    - ~Fractions with equivalent fractions
    - ~Options for prioritizing
    - ~Preferences for voting
    - ~Similarities and differences by their placement in Venn diagrams
    - ~Students into work groups

Alternate Text Vocabulary   (4–8)

Students are motivated by texts that interest them—and, unfortunately, these are not always the ones schools have available. This activity gives students a chance to use their personal interests to reinforce the classroom texts. Alternate Text Vocabulary provides a creative structure that reinforces new vocabulary words and improves retention.

How To

1. Write the following as a list on the board or on an overhead transparency: sports magazine, teen-fashion magazine, environmental/nature magazine, art magazine, sales ad, children's dictionary, comics, school announcement, cookbook, poetry collection, health handbook.

2. After teaching a new vocabulary word and its meaning, tell the students that they are to imagine that they are reading an alternate text from the list. Ask how the word might be defined and used in context in the alternate text. Provide one or more examples, such as:

    Word: *Acid*

    In cookbook: *"Do not add extra tomatoes to this recipe. Tomatoes are very acidic, and the additional acid may make the recipe sour or corrode your saucepan."*

    Word: *Base*

    In sports magazine: *"Remember that challenging workouts will cause you to sweat and stink. Use lots of deodorant—it includes a base that will neutralize body odor."*

3. Allow students to work in pairs, choose an alternate text, and define the word in context.

4. Call on students to share their definitions. As students listen, they will hear the vocabulary word used and defined several times—great for retention!

Variations

- Ask students for suggestions for other alternate texts to add to the list.
- Allow students to act out their definitions, as if they were doing a commercial, a cooking demonstration, or a reality television show.
- Instead of alternate texts, suggest that students consider alternate settings. For example, students might describe how a word could be used at the zoo, the mall, the soccer field, or a toy store.

Tip

☆ Assign heterogeneous partnerships so that students who need support are paired with students who are strong linguistically.

Text Retell Cards   (2–8)

When a student can retell what she has read, we know that her comprehension is satisfactory. When she can retell it from another person's perspective, she has had the opportunity to tap into higher-level-thinking skills. Text Retell Cards encourage students to consider the text from another perspective and retell the material in that way. This strategy also provides listeners with multiple repetitions of the content, thus increasing retention for all.

Materials

Text Retell Cards (see reproducible, page 140)

Card stock

How To

1. Make copies of the cards, cut them apart, and glue them to a piece of card stock to make them more durable (or laminate them).

2. When students are about to read as a group, pass out the cards to a few students who you feel are ready for the challenge. Quietly review the directions on the cards with them.

3. At an appropriate time during the lesson, call on one of the students to read his card aloud and then retell the content as directed. Give corrective feedback if necessary.

Variation

● Direction Retell Cards (see reproducible, page 141) can be used to ensure that all students understand teacher directions. Copy and cut apart the cards. Distribute one or two cards to the class prior to giving lengthy directions. Call on students to retell the directions to the entire class.

Tip

☆ Provide students with a time limit for their retelling—30 seconds is usually adequate.

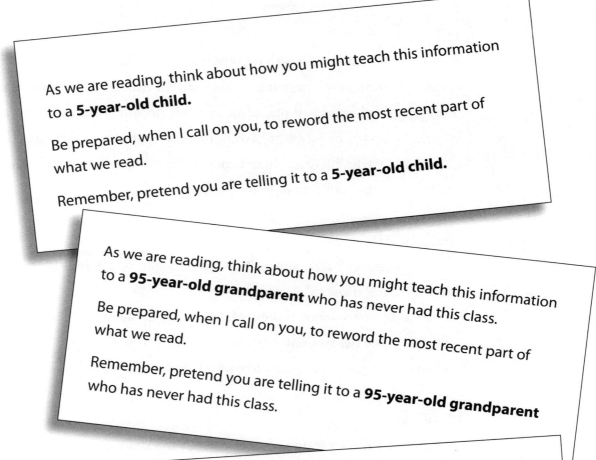

As we are reading, think about how you might teach this information to a **5-year-old child.**

Be prepared, when I call on you, to reword the most recent part of what we read.

Remember, pretend you are telling it to a **5-year-old child.**

As we are reading, think about how you might teach this information to a **95-year-old grandparent** who has never had this class.

Be prepared, when I call on you, to reword the most recent part of what we read.

Remember, pretend you are telling it to a **95-year-old grandparent** who has never had this class.

As we are reading, think about how you might teach this information if you were a **cartoon character from television** (Bart Simpson, Spider-Man, SpongeBob, etc.).

Be prepared, when I call on you, to reword the most recent part of what we read.

Remember, pretend you are **a cartoon character.**

Graphic Organizer Puzzles (1–8)

Memory research indicates that graphic organizers are effective tools in helping students comprehend, organize, and retain information. This is because the content is condensed and placed in a specific location on the page, tapping into the episodic, or location-driven, memory path (Sprenger, pg. 51). Graphic Organizer Puzzles increase these benefits by adding physical movement and flexibility to the traditional graphic approach.

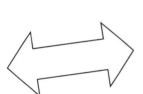

Materials

Graphic Organizer Puzzle Shapes (see reproducible, pages 142–143)

Adhesive-backed Velcro

Shallow box, such as shoe box or plastic storage container

File folders, one per student

Water-based, wipe-off markers, one per student

How To

1. Laminate the reproducible and cut out the shapes.

2. Apply a small piece of the hook side of the Velcro to the back of each of the shapes, and place them into a shallow container.

3. Apply three 6-inch strips of the loop side of the Velcro to the inside of each file folder (see illustration).

4. Distribute a file folder and marker to each student.

5. Direct the students to choose shapes they would like to use in their file folders, and model which shapes might be appropriate for the assigned task. For example, when brainstorming ideas for a paragraph, it might be

best to use one large shape for the main idea and several smaller shapes for supporting details.

6. Demonstrate how to write the ideas on the shapes and attach them to the Velcro in the folder. Then show the students how they can organize and rearrange their ideas as they develop them. For example, in the initial brainstorming, the supporting details might surround the main idea. But as students get ready to put the ideas into a paragraph, they can move them into a sequence they like best.

7. Direct the students to store their work in the file folders until they have finished the writing or learning assignment.

Variation

● Instead of using Velcro, students can apply a small piece of tape or sticky tack onto the back of the shape they will use, then stick it to the inside of the folder.

Tip

☆ Some teachers laminate the folders so they will last longer. This also allows students to write on the folders without destroying them.

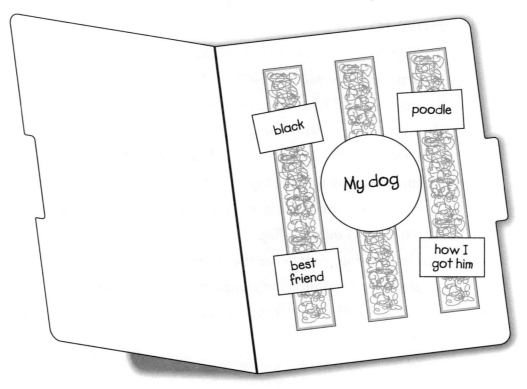

Boomerang Bookmarks (2–6)

Some students become engrossed in their reading, while others read more superficially. Boomerang Bookmarks are tools that assist students to stay engaged and attend to the content as they read. In addition, when students return to their reading at a later time, they can refer to the bookmarks to remind them of the content. Because the bookmarks are available in three different levels, teachers can match them to a student's readiness level.

Materials

Boomerang Bookmarks (see reproducibles, pages 144-146)

Water-based, wipe-off markers (if laminating)

How To

1. Decide whether or not to laminate the bookmarks. Laminating allows students to write with wipe-off markers and reuse the bookmarks. The bookmarks do not need to be laminated if a permanent product is desired (for a portfolio or to send home).

2. Determine the appropriate level of bookmark for each student.

3. Introduce the Boomerang Bookmarks to the students within leveled reading groups, and explain that they will be writing on their bookmarks in response to their reading.

4. Demonstrate how to use the bookmark appropriate to the level of the group, and monitor the groups during the first experience. If students are successful with their use, then direct students to use them at independent reading times.

5. Have students keep their places with their bookmarks in longer reading material. When returning to their reading, they should quickly review any information they've previously written on the bookmark.

Tip

☆ To protect student self-esteem, the bookmarks are not marked with a level. The less complex bookmark has visual cues built in, and the highest level bookmark asks students to develop questions as they read. All three bookmarks allow for variation in assigned quantity.

Name _Justin_

Directions:
Write a question for __5__ of the question words below.

Who does Mrs. Mooney ask for help?

What can she do to not lose her purse again?

When

Where do you think the purse is?

Why is Mrs. Mooney worried?

How would you feel in her place?

Name _Amanda_

Directions:
Answer __4__ of the questions below.

Who is it about?
Mrs. Mooney

What happened?
She lost her purse.

When did it happen?

Where is the story taking place?
At the Mall

Why did it happen?

How did the character feel?
confused

Make a Connection (1–8)

Learning becomes more meaningful when learners can connect the content to their own life experiences. This is true in all content areas and at all ages. To encourage students to make these connections and share them with the class, try Make a Connection. This simple strategy employs a tactile approach to entice students to make connections between the content and their previous experiences and knowledge.

Materials

8½ x 11-inch sheet of white paper

2 x 11-inch strip of colored paper

Stapler

How To

1. Orient the white paper in landscape position. Across the top of it, print the curriculum area, such as "Math."

2. Print the word "Connections" on the colored strip of paper and staple it onto the sheet of paper, covering the bottom two inches of the sheet. Attach a single staple to each end of the colored strip (see illustration).

3. Hang the sheet of paper low enough on a wall to be accessible to the students, and place a stapler nearby.

4. Explain to the class that when a student has a connection between the content and a personal experience, she will be allowed to come to the board and "Make a Connection." This means that the student can attach a staple to the Connections slip and share the connection with the rest of the class.

5. As appropriate, ask questions of the student to lead the class in understanding the type of connection (text-to-self, text-to-text, etc.) and in expanding on the experience.

Variations

- If you would like to encourage students to develop specific types of connections, write the specific type on the colored strip. For example, if the goal is to help students make connections between the book they are reading and other books they have read, write "Text-to-Text Connections" on the colored paper.
- If you are teaching several different classes of students, set up a sheet of paper for each class. Mark the top of the paper with the class name or period. Hang all the papers in an accessible place. As you use the Make a Connection strategy with each class, the students will begin to notice how the other groups are doing. This can add a healthy serving of motivation to make more connections.

Tip

☆ Consider developing and explaining some guidelines for the quality of connections you want shared. Guidelines might suggest that students share connections that are relevant, brief, and timely.

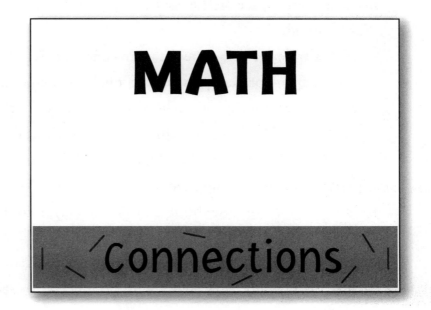

Group Graffiti   (K–8)

Graffiti is a public form of expression with negative connotations. Usually graffiti is done illegally and with the purpose of defacing public property. But it also can be an artistic way of expressing strong opinions and ideas—summarizing them into succinct verbal and visual messages. Because linguistic and nonlinguistic summarization is a critical skill for students, graffiti makes sense for the classroom!

Materials

12-foot piece of butcher paper, or two 6-foot pieces

Wide markers or crayons

Pictures of buildings with graffiti (optional)

How To

1. Clear a large space on the floor in the classroom, and place the paper on the ground.

2. With a wide marker, write the main concept being studied in the center of the paper. For example, "utopia" might be a concept in a literature unit. For younger students, it might be "the world" or "citizenship."

3. Talk with students about graffiti. If possible, show them pictures of different buildings with graffiti. Discuss the differences between meaningful graffiti and simple vandalism.

4. Have the students each bring a marker or crayon to the paper and sit down around the perimeter of the butcher paper.

5. Direct the students to draw pictures and use words or phrases to express their feelings and knowledge about the concept. For example, if utopia is

the theme, a student might write the word *possible* with question marks all around it. Someone next to him might draw a single stick figure to indicate that each person's utopia would be different.

6. When finished with the Group Graffiti, discuss various contributions and then hang it on a wall in the classroom, in the hallway, or, if permitted, on the outside of the school building.

Variation

- Group Graffiti can be done in smaller groups with smaller pieces of paper. Students should still be asked to work on the floor, as it fosters a more creative, less constrained approach to the task.

Tips

☆ If the weather is nice, move the butcher paper outdoors, tape it to a wall or concrete surface, and work on it there.

☆ Help the students to understand that graffiti does not need to look neat—words and pictures can be written and drawn from different angles and even upside down.

4 x 6 Posters   (2–8)

Differentiation according to student readiness allows teachers to meet students at their individual instructional levels. While this has great benefits for students, it can also bring with it the risk of embarrassing less-able students. The 4 x 6 Posters strategy allows students to be exposed to all the learning levels in the room, with the protection of anonymity.

Materials

Sheets of poster board or butcher paper

How To

1. Develop six tasks that represent the content you have taught. Include two tasks for students at a lower readiness level, two in a mid-range, and two for students who are most able. Do not mark the tasks in any way that will make the levels obvious. (The illustration *has* been marked for level as a demonstration only.)

2. After printing out several copies of the tasks, cut them into individual strips of paper.

3. Hand each student a task suitable to her readiness level. (Because there are so many different tasks, the levels will be less obvious to students than if there were only three.)

4. Assign the students to cooperative learning groups, with four students per group. Each group should be heterogeneous, with at least one student from each level represented.

5. Provide each group with a large piece of poster board or butcher paper. Direct the students to divide it into four sections and to sit around the board or paper so that they each have easy access to one section of it.

6. Have the students glue their task strip onto the top of their section of the paper. The strips will be facing in different directions.

7. Have each student complete his task in the space under his task strip. Encourage the students to talk as they work, showing each other their efforts. This will allow them to be exposed to the other leveled tasks.

8. Display the 4 x 6 posters for students to browse.

Variation

● If poster board or butcher paper is not available, have students work on individual sheets of paper and tape them together into a large rectangle when completed.

Tips

☆ Lower-level tasks should have very specific directions and prompts. Be sure to include page numbers where appropriate. Higher-level tasks should be more open ended.

☆ Wander around the room as you hand out tasks, being sure to make it look like random assignments, rather than based on ability level.

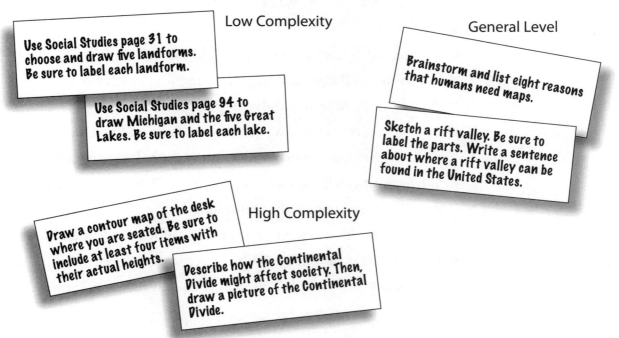

Low Complexity

Use Social Studies page 31 to choose and draw five landforms. Be sure to label each landform.

Use Social Studies page 94 to draw Michigan and the five Great Lakes. Be sure to label each lake.

General Level

Brainstorm and list eight reasons that humans need maps.

Sketch a rift valley. Be sure to label the parts. Write a sentence about where a rift valley can be found in the United States.

High Complexity

Draw a contour map of the desk where you are seated. Be sure to include at least four items with their actual heights.

Describe how the Continental Divide might affect society. Then, draw a picture of the Continental Divide.

Glove Balloons (K–5)

Balloons bring smiles and positive energy to any occasion. This "feel-good" effect has been linked to increased retention! Using the Glove Balloons strategy will ensure that these same benefits are linked to your classroom curriculum standards.

Materials

Permanent marker

Disposable rubber or latex exam gloves (available from the school nurse or from grocery and drug stores)

How To

1. Use the marker to write on the fingers of the glove. Depending on the content, choose five concepts to write. For example:
   - Who, What, When, Where, Why
   - 1, 2, 3, 4, 5
   - Setting, Character, Action, Main Idea, Detail
   - Renaissance, Baroque, Classical, Romantic, Contemporary
   - Noun, Verb, Adjective, Adverb, Preposition

2. Blow up the glove, as if it was a balloon, and tie a knot to secure it.

3. Explain to the students that you will toss the balloon to someone. The recipient must catch the balloon by a finger. Whichever finger the student grabs will be the content she will respond to.

4. Demonstrate with a student. For example, if the student catches a "Who" finger, she might be asked a "Who" question about the story the class read, or to generate her own "Who" question about the story for her classmates

to answer. In music class, if a student catches a "Romantic" finger, she might need to name a characteristic, composer, or piece of music from the Romantic era.

5. After each response, that student can toss the balloon back to the teacher or to another student.

Variation

- Glove Balloons can be used with small groups. Blow up one glove for each group and have students stand in a circle and toss the balloon to each other.

Tips

☆ Lead off with open-ended questions. These usually make it less obvious that an easier question has been asked of a student who is not ready for something more complex.

☆ Next time you have a scheduled doctor's appointment, ask for a few exam gloves to use in your classroom.

☆ If any students have latex allergies, be sure to use latex-free gloves.

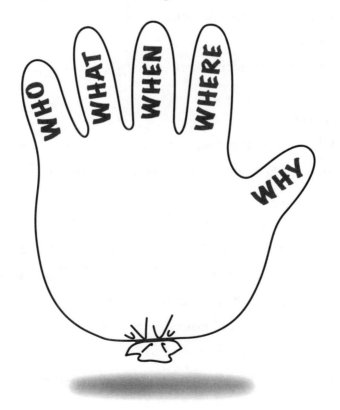

Millionaire Game (2–6)

Effective teachers use a variety of methods for assessing student learning. While some of these take place after instruction, good teachers also use assessment techniques during instruction to ensure that students understand the content as it is presented. Unfortunately, as students get older, they become easily embarrassed if they do not understand something and may be hesitant to admit it. The Millionaire Game, based on the popular television show, provides students with a fun, nonthreatening way to give instant feedback to the teacher.

Materials

Millionaire Game (see reproducible, page 147)

Calculators

Water-based, wipe-off markers

How To

1. Make a copy of the reproducible, laminate it, and hang it on the board.
2. Provide two students with calculators and the formula for determining percentage.
3. Ask students if they have seen the *Millionaire Game* on television, and describe it if any students aren't familiar with the program. Remind them that participants have a "lifeline," which allows them to ask the audience's opinion about the answer to a question. The audience's answers are tallied instantaneously and posted as a bar graph.
4. Explain that it is important for teachers to know how students are feeling about their understanding of a lesson. Therefore, once or twice throughout

the lesson, students will be asked to choose A, B, C, or D as a response: A = Totally Understand It, B = Think I Get It, C = Confused, D = Totally Lost.

5. At a point during the lesson when it is unclear if students are grasping the instruction, prompt students to choose, in turn, A, B, C, or D.

6. As students raise their hands in response to A, count the hands. Tell the number to the students with calculators and ask them to figure the percentage of the class who responded A.

7. Have another student use a wipe-off marker to enter the percentage as a bar above "A" on the reproducible.

8. Repeat Steps 5–7 for B, C, and D.

9. Summarize the data for the students and decide how to adjust your instruction accordingly.

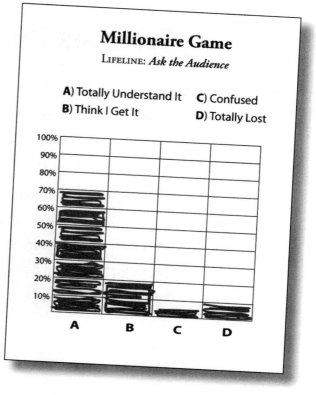

Variation

● Adjust the A, B, C, and D responses to read "Strongly Agree, Agree, Disagree, and Neutral." Generate statements about the content and then ask students to respond to show their level of agreement. For example, in a lesson on the American Revolution, the statement might be, "The colonists were right to break laws they felt were tyrannical."

Tip

☆ Choose students to assist with the calculator and the graphing based on needs and abilities. These roles provide students with excellent practice on math skills but should be accomplished quickly, as the class will be waiting to see their results.

T-Notes Plus (5–8)

Note taking, an essential skill for student achievement, is usually introduced as students prepare to enter middle school. Many formats abound. T-Notes is a format that builds upon standard note taking by adding illustrations and concluding with a summary statement. These two extra features are extremely helpful for struggling learners but valuable practice for all students. Add to these the "Plus" feature for reviewing T-Notes, and students have a solid learning strategy in T-Notes Plus that will carry them through the rest of their school years.

Materials

Manila folders

Scissors

How To

1. Model for students how to format their paper for T-Notes (see Illustration A.).

2. As you lecture on the content, use the overhead projector to demonstrate note taking with words, by drawing quick pictures and by generating a summary statement (see Illustration B.). Direct students to take T-Notes, following your model but developing their own pictures and words.

3. When students have finished their T-Notes, provide each one with a manila folder and a pair of scissors. Show them how to draw the horizontal and vertical lines. Have them write "My Notes," "My Drawings," and "My Summary" on the front of the folder (see Illustration C.) and then cut the folder along the dashed cut lines.

4. Have students fold the front cover (see Illustration C.) back along the vertical center fold line, then up along the horizontal fold line near the bottom, and return the folder to its original flat position.

5. Show students how to slide their T-Notes into the folder so that the bottom edge aligns with that of the folder. Explain the T-Notes Plus study strategy:

   ■ First, try to generate a summary of the material. Then flip up Section 1 of the folder to see if you were correct. Is your summary similar to the one written under Section 1?

   ■ Second, fold back Section 2 and look at the drawings. Do you remember what they stand for?

   ■ Third, review the notes under Section 3 to see if your recall was accurate. Reread the notes to find important details.

Variation

● Suggest that students use the back of their paper to write down any questions they have about the content.

Tip

☆ Allow students to make two folders—one for school and one for home. Encourage them to use the T-Notes Plus strategy at home when studying for a test.

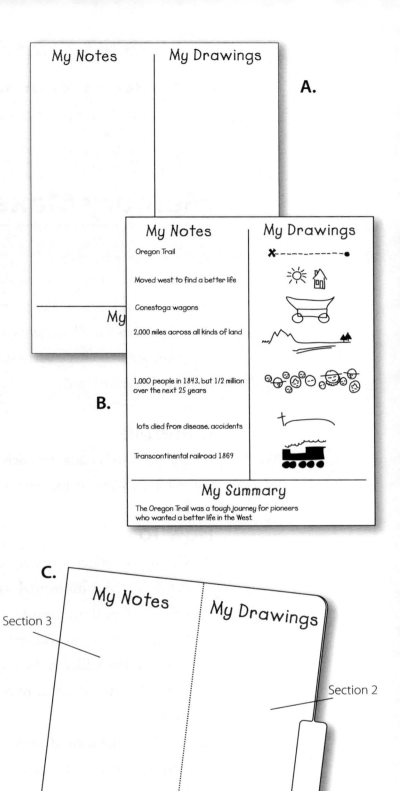

Memory Makers (K–8)

Rote memorization comes easily to some students . . . and not so easily to others. Strategies for making rote practice more interactive will increase the retention rates for all students. Memory Makers, simple hands-on devices, allow students to check accuracy as they practice spelling words, definitions, or other basic material.

Materials

Laminated manila folder for each student (prepared as described)

Water-based, wipe-off marker for each student

How To

1. Orient the folder vertically, divide the front of the folder into fourths, and cut it into four horizontal strips, keeping them attached to the folder at the left edge (see illustration).

2. Open the top strip and, using the marker, write a spelling word on the inside of the folder at the top.

3. Show the students how to cover up the spelling word by closing the top strip.

4. Fold back the second strip and demonstrate how to write the spelling word from memory in the second space.

5. Check accuracy by opening the first strip.

6. Repeat this procedure in the third and fourth spaces using another word.

7. Provide the students with a folder, marker, and spelling list for practice with the Memory Makers.

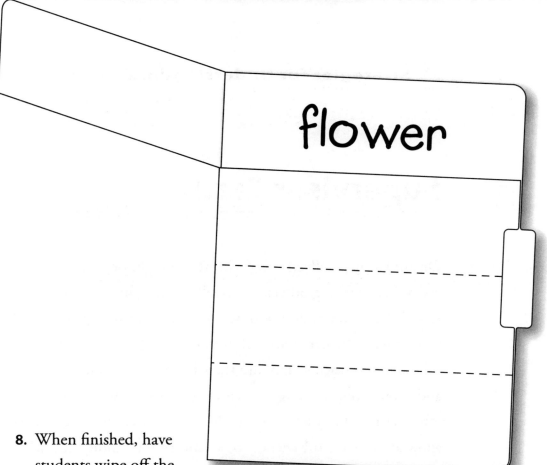

8. When finished, have students wipe off the Memory Makers so they will be ready for future use.

Variations

- Memory Makers can be used to practice definitions, math equations, or any other brief content that must be memorized.
- Instead of laminating the Memory Makers, just cut the folders as directed above. Have the students place a piece of paper inside the folder and practice on the paper.
- Folders can also be used as Work Masks (Beninghof, 1993) to cut down on visual distraction. A student can place his work sheet inside the folder and cover up three-fourths of the page as he works on one part of the page.

Tip

☆ Memory Makers are great to have at a spelling or vocabulary center. Make just five or six folders, depending on the number of students typically assigned to a center.

Supervisor Cards (4–8)

One of the most effective ways for retaining information is to teach it to others. When teaching others, we usually review the material several times, explain it in different ways, discuss other views, and answer questions. All these interactions with the material reinforce our knowledge and understanding. Successful classroom teachers tap into these benefits by implementing peer tutoring and cooperative learning in their classrooms. However, struggling students are often relegated to the role of receiver, rather than teacher. Supervisor Cards allow all students the chance to benefit from teaching others.

Materials

Supervisor Cards (see reproducible, page 148)

How To

1. Make copies of the reproducible, cut them apart, and laminate the cards.
2. Choose a lesson that will require students to work in small groups or as individuals to solve a problem. For example, in a math class, students might be experimenting to figure out the equation for finding the perimeter of a rectangle.
3. Write the correct answer on the Supervisor Cards, as well as any explanatory information (see illustration).
4. Hand out the cards to two or three students who might benefit from the extra support and "supervisor" practice.
5. Direct these students to wander around the room, checking in with their peers, acting as a supervisor. Specifically, they should ask questions, check answers against the answer on the Supervisor Cards, and provide assistance.

Be clear that they are expected to use the information on the Supervisor Cards to help others find the correct answer.

Variations

- To stimulate higher-level thinking, place creative questions on the Supervisor Cards and direct students to ask these of the groups and record their answers.
- Younger students might enjoy wearing a badge that says "Supervisor" as they circulate around the room. These can be made from name-tag badges that are available at office supply stores.

Tips

☆ Save your clear-plastic name-tag badges that you receive at educational conferences to use as supervisor badges for younger students.

☆ Supervisor Cards work well with students who can correctly read the material written on the card. Struggling readers will be more successful if paired with a stronger reader.

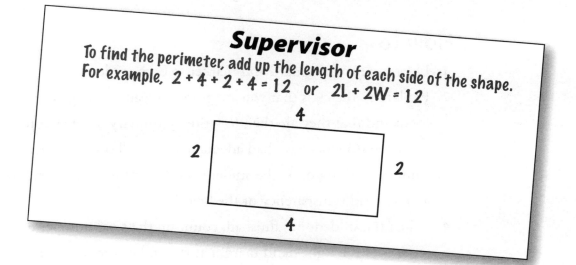

Subtraction Summary (3–8)

The ability to summarize has been identified as one of the skills that will most positively affect learning (Marzano, et al., 2001). Yet many students do not know how to summarize effectively. They may meander on and on, adding lots of insignificant detail. Or, perhaps, they miss the main idea altogether. Subtraction Summary provides repeated practice with summarizing while also providing repeated review of the content being studied.

Materials

Whiteboard for each student

Marker for each student

10 playing cards, with the value of each card being between 6 and 13 (There will be multiples of some of the higher cards.)

How To

1. Distribute a whiteboard and marker to each student.

2. Explain to the class that you are going to read a passage from the text to them and that they are then to write a summary of what you read.

3. After the students have had adequate time, call on one to read her summary out loud. As the student speaks, write down every word on an overhead transparency or the board.

4. When the student has finished, count up the total number of words, and write it in the right-hand margin at the end of the summary. For example, the first summary might have 35 words.

5. Holding the deck of cards in your hands, ask another student to remove one of the cards. Subtract the card value from the total word count of the

original summary. In our example, if a student removes the 9 card, write the problem 35 − 9 = 26 in the margin of the transparency.

6. Explain to the students that they are to summarize again but in exactly that number of words (26). They can use the original statement and just erase some of the unnecessary words, or they can start fresh.

7. After adequate time has passed, call on a student who has the correct number of words in a summary. Again, record every word the student reads.

8. Repeat steps 5–7 until the final summary is fewer than eight words.

9. Discuss the activity, drawing the students' attention to the fact that they were able to become more and more succinct in their summarizations.

Variations

- Subtraction Summary can be used to summarize almost any learning that takes place in the classroom—a lecture, a class activity, or a video.
- Students can do Subtraction Summary as an individual practice. In this case, each student will need his own set of cards.
- If playing cards aren't available, use numbered slips of paper instead.
- Students can work in heterogeneous partners to develop their summaries. This may be a helpful support for students who struggle with summarizing.
- Choose a few words that will likely be in an effective summary statement. Write them where students cannot see them. Challenge students to see if they can develop a summary that includes the "secret summary words."

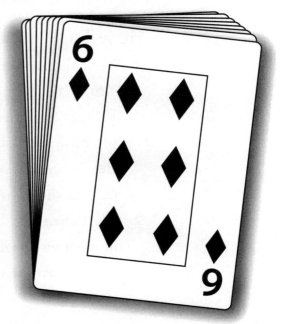

Tips

☆ If whiteboards are not available, students can use notebook paper.

☆ If a student shares a "summary" that is not a strong example, use the opportunity to review and discuss what makes an effective summary.

Shrink It (3–6)

Identifying the main idea in a large amount of reading material can be a challenge for many students. They need to be able to remove the "fluff" but leave the essential elements. The Shrink It strategy provides students with a powerful visual model of this process and allows them to practice shrinking the larger material down to its essence.

Materials

Large plastic garbage bag

Large bed comforter

Vacuum cleaner with hose attachment (borrow from custodian)

Whiteboard for each student

Marker for each student

24-inch length of yarn for each student

How To

1. While the students are watching, place the comforter inside the plastic bag. Position the hose in the bag, grasp the bag closed around it, and turn on the vacuum cleaner. As the vacuum sucks the air out of the bag, the comforter will shrink to approximately 10 percent of its original size. The visual effect is very powerful! Students will be able to observe how a large, bulky item has shrunk to a small, very compact article.

2. Ask students for their observations. Discuss the concept of "shrinking" information down to its main idea or essence (getting rid of the fluff). Tell students that they will have a chance to practice this.

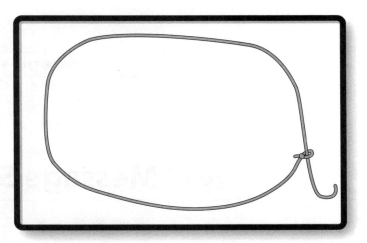

3. Provide each student with a whiteboard, marker, and piece of yarn, and show how to loop the yarn so that it forms a large circle with a slipknot. The goal is to have a circle that can be pulled smaller and smaller.

4. Direct the students to place their string circles on the whiteboards and to make their circles almost as large as the boards (see illustration).

5. Read aloud a passage from a novel or text that will serve as a practice piece for Shrink It, and then model the activity using your overhead projector. Starting with a large string circle, write a summary of the passage within the circle. Ask the students to do the same.

6. Call on students to share their summaries, and then have them erase their boards. Show the students how to pull on their yarn to shrink the size of their circle, and ask them to shrink theirs to about half the original size.

7. Within that smaller circle, have students again write a summary of the passage but with less "fluff." Then ask them to share their process for reducing the content. Repeat the steps with another passage.

Variation

- Instead of individual whiteboards, have students use writing paper. Rather than erasing their previous summaries, they can look back to determine which words or phrases to eliminate. When finished, students can turn in their papers for their writing portfolios.

Tip

☆ Some students are clever enough to figure out that the size of their print will affect what fits in the circle. Remind them that the goal is to use fewer words in each successive summary.

Text Message Summary (3–8)

Students are fascinated with the technological gadgets available in our communities. Many of them own cell phones, computers, iPods, pdas . . . and more! Teachers who use technology as a hook for learning tap into strong motivation and interest. Text Message Summary is an instructional activity that uses a familiar concept to practice summarizing the main idea of a reading passage or experience.

Materials

"Cell phone" (see reproducible, page 149) for each student

How To

1. Make copies of the reproducible. If desired, laminate for repeated use.

2. Ask students to share their prior knowledge regarding text messaging. Student input might include comments such as "It's fast," "It uses minutes," "People use abbreviations to make it shorter." Be sure that the discussion emphasizes the need to keep messages short and to the point.

3. Explain to students that we can use the same skills in school that we use in text messaging. Point out that the ability to summarize succinctly is an important skill for learning and sharing with others.

4. Read a short passage from a text. Model for the students how it might be summarized for a text message. For example, "Pioneers had little time for fun, but sometimes they turned their work into a party. Whenever there was a big job to be completed in a short time, they invited neighbors to a special party called a bee. Bees were held to husk corn, build houses or barns, or sew quilts. There was always plenty of food, music, and some-

times dancing, too—when the work was finished, of course!" (Sinnot, 1999, p. 16) The text message summary example might read as follows: "bee=pioneer work parT"

5. Provide each student with a copy of the Text Message Summary reproducible. Direct the students to read a selection from the text and summarize the passage in the text box on the cell phone.

6. Ask for volunteers to share their text message aloud.

Variations

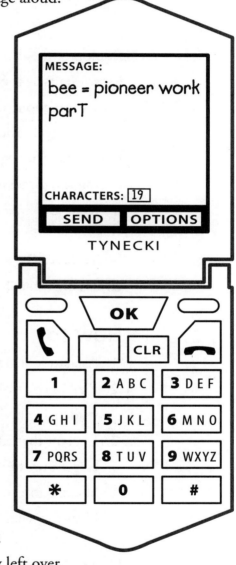

- Older students may have their own cell phones with them in school. Ask for two volunteers to demonstrate a live text messaging of a summary of the passage.

- Younger students may enjoy "owning" their own cell phone. Copy the reproducible, cut out the phone shape, and laminate it. Glue it to a piece of card stock, foam board, or Styrofoam. Give each student a "cell phone" and direct her to write her text message summary on the phone with a wipe-off marker.

- Compare text messages to telegraph messages. With telegraphs, the writer had to pay for each letter or punctuation mark. If available, show an example of an authentic telegraph. Give students play money and set a price per letter. Have students write telegraph summaries, with a goal of having a clear summary and money left over.

Tip

☆ Be sensitive to the economic variations within the class. Not all students will have access to the same technology in their homes.

Sweet Sheets (3–8)

Book groups, also referred to as literature circles, are a beneficial experience for students as they study literature. Book groups allow students to engage in discussion about what they are reading, making it meaningful to them on a personal level. The students who might benefit the most, however, from this type of experience may also be the ones who struggle with deciding what to say during the discussions. Rather than allowing them to sit back and just listen, try using the Sweet Sheets strategy to provide some support.

Materials

Copies of Sweet Sheets (see reproducibles, pages 150–151)

How To

1. Ask students to get into their book groups.
2. Place a copy of a Sweet Sheet in the center of each group, so that all the students can view it from wherever they are seated.
3. Explain that there are times, for everyone, when we might need a little help to get our thinking and conversations started—and that's what the Sweet Sheet is for: to help them during their discussions if they are in need of ideas for what to say.

Variations

- Consider sending a Sweet Sheet home with students. Encourage parents to use it when they are reading a book with their child.
- Use a Sweet Sheet during whole-group discussions of books by copying the reproducible onto a transparency and placing it on an overhead projector.

- A Sweet Sheet can be developed for any content discussion. For example, in science, a Sweet Sheet might include several statement starters about the scientific process, the surprises of an experiment, or predictions.

Tips

☆ Be sure to make it clear that all learners occasionally have difficulty thinking of things to say. A Sweet Sheet should not be viewed by students as being only for the struggling students in the group.

☆ Preteach some of these discussion starters to students who might struggle with on-the-spot thinking.

☆ A Sweet Sheet is especially helpful for students who are learning English as a second language and may not yet have learned some of the necessary vocabulary for a literature circle.

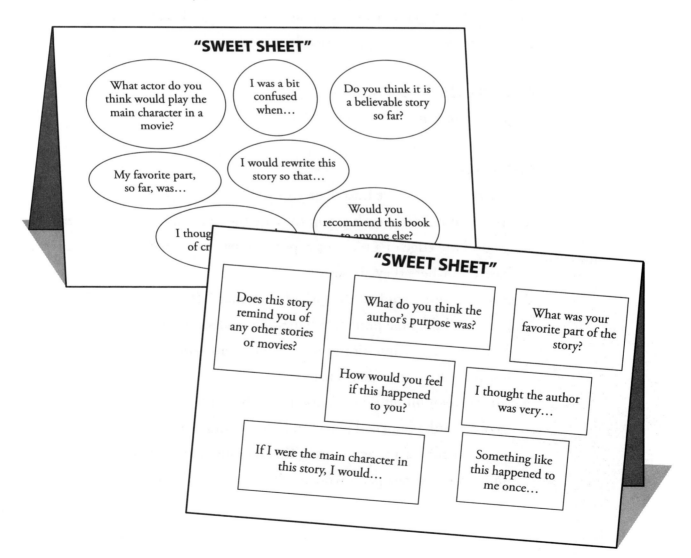

Participation Punch (1–8)

Cooperative learning is a valuable method for enhancing student learning beyond the academic curriculum. The skills needed to interact collaboratively will be useful in all walks of life. There are many times, however, when the participation in learning groups is imbalanced. Students who are not socially adept may be passive or might be unaware of dominating the group activity. Participation Punch is a strategy that can be used to balance participation in cooperative activities in any curriculum area.

Materials

Single-hole punch

How To

1. Have students move into their groups.

2. Assign someone in each group to write the first names of the students around the edge of a piece of paper. The names should be written in order, based on where they are seated.

3. Assign another student the task of "puncher." This student will have the paper and the hole punch. Whenever a student in the group participates in any way—asks a question, makes a comment—the puncher will punch a hole next to that student's name.

4. After several minutes have passed, ask the students to pause. Direct them to observe the punched paper and silently draw conclusions about the group members' participation. (This is done silently so that students do not publicly embarrass peers who are dominating or being passive.)

5. As the students resume their group discussions, wander around the room just observing. Where appropriate, stop and talk with groups about ways to increase the balance in their participation.

Variations

- Participation Punch can be used with whole-class activities as well. The trick is to start with the right piece (or pieces) of paper. For example, if students are seated in rows, cut strips of paper so that each row is on a separate strip, making it easy to punch a hole next to participating students' names.
- If a hole punch is not available, use a stapler, or simply direct students to place a check mark by the name.

Tip

☆ Assign the job of "puncher" to the most tactile student in the group. It will give him wonderful tactile input!

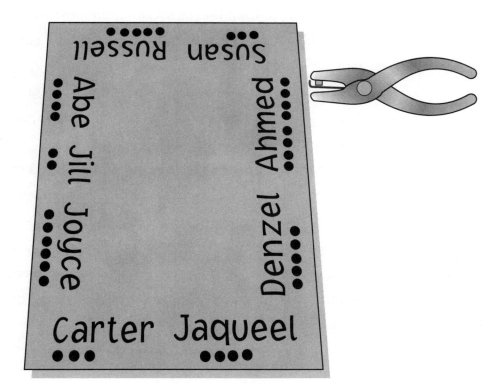

Bubble-Wrap Response (K–5)

Large-group discussions are a common component of today's classrooms. Discussions allow students the opportunity to make meaning of their learning, hear other opinions, and practice verbal skills. Like teacher lectures, discussions rely heavily on auditory input. Bubble-Wrap Response is a simple strategy for incorporating tactile input into classroom conversations.

Materials

Pieces of bubble-wrap packaging material

How To

1. Cut the bubble wrap into strips containing five unpopped bubbles each. (To avoid student complaints, make sure that all students receive strips with the same number of bubbles.)

2. Hand out the bubble-wrap strips to the students, and give them permission to pop one of their bubbles. This will give them practice and avoid the problem of unanticipated pops.

3. During the discussion or lecture, ask a close-ended question of the students. For example, "Do you think that the author's purpose is to inform the reader?"

4. Tell the students to pop a bubble if the answer is "yes" and to keep silent if the answer is "no." Sit back and listen to the symphony of sound!

5. After bubbles have been popped in response to the question, choose students to elaborate on their answers.

Variations

- Encourage higher-level thinking by asking students to generate statements for Bubble-Wrap Response.
- When reading to students, direct them to pop a bubble every time they hear an action verb (or other part of speech).
- In math class, ask students to pop a bubble every time you show a picture of a quadrilateral (or triangle, circle, etc.).
- In art or music class, ask students to pop a bubble every time you share an example from the Renaissance Period.
- Use Bubble-Wrap Response as a motivational system. Obtain one large piece of bubble wrap and hang it in the front of the room. When a student is deserving of recognition or reward, allow her to go up and pop a few bubbles.

Tips

☆ If there is a student in the class with poor fine-motor strength, offer him a tack or pin to use for popping bubbles.

☆ Ask parents to save the bubble wrap that comes with packages they receive and to donate it to the class.

☆ Bubble wrap comes in different sizes. The medium or large bubbles are more effective than the small ones.

☆ Bubble-Wrap Response proves to be a great energizer for students as they listen to all the popping sounds. Use it at a time when students are in need of a little pick-me-up.

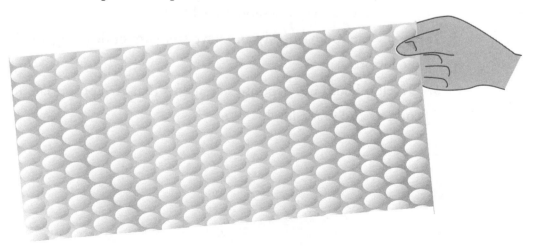

Stand in Response (K–8)

Kinesthetic interactions lead to the most efficient and effective learning for many students. Therefore, teachers need to have a handful of quick and easy kinesthetic activities that apply to a wide variety of content. Stand in Response (Beninghof, 1998) is one of the simplest! This strategy needs no specific materials or preparation and can be used at any grade level and with any content.

How To

1. As you are teaching, ask students to "Stand up if . . .

   . . . you have a connection."

   . . . you know the answer."

   . . . you agree with another student's answer."

   . . . you disagree with me (the teacher)."

   . . . you have ever…"

   . . . the word *cat* starts with the letter *c*."

   . . . 5 x 5 = 25."

   . . . *azul* means 'blue.'"

   . . . the capital of Colorado is Denver."

2. Survey the room quickly and have students sit down again. Continue with the lesson.

3. Develop Stand in Response statements that are appropriate to the current content and grade level.

Variations

- If there is a student in a wheelchair, try this variation: Have students turn to their right or left (standing or seated) in response to a question. The student in a wheelchair can also turn (or be turned) like her classmates.

- In some countries, affirmation and approval is sometimes noted by stomping one's feet repeatedly. Explain this custom to students and direct them to use this response in class. It will give strong kinesthetic input and reinforce the response with a rousing auditory signal!

Tips

☆ Research suggests that attention and retention diminish after 20 minutes of instruction if there have been no opportunities to move. So use the Stand in Response technique at least every 20 minutes.

☆ Design statements that will get most of the students out of their seats. For example, "Stand up if you have ever seen a pyramid" is likely to get most students up, as opposed to "Stand up if you have ever been to Egypt."

Voice Bells (K–5)

"Learning—everyone, everyday." This mission statement, adopted by a Colorado elementary school, is an extraordinary goal for teachers at any grade level—and an extraordinary challenge. Even the best teachers sometimes realize, at the end of a day, that they didn't have a chance to connect with one or more of their students during that day. Voice Bells is a musical method for tracking which students have had a chance to actively participate and have their voices heard throughout the day.

Materials

Metal jingle bell for each student

Permanent marker

Adhesive Velcro

Fabric or poster board

How To

1. With a permanent marker, label each bell with the name or initials of a student in the class. (Some teachers assign numbers to students for cubbies, lockers, or textbooks. If students have a number assigned to them, bells can be labeled with these numbers so that they can be reused each year.)

2. Adhere a small piece of Velcro to the back of each bell, and adhere the matching pieces of Velcro to a piece of fabric or poster board. The Velcro can be placed randomly, leaving at least two inches between each piece.

3. Label the fabric or poster "Our voices have been heard!" (see illustration) and hang it low enough on a wall to be accessible to students. Store the bells nearby.

4. Explain to the students that each of their voices is important in your class and that throughout the day, they will have opportunities to share their stories, connections, and opinions. When they have a turn to share, they will get to pick up their bell and attach it to the wall hanging.

5. During the course of the day, survey the wall hanging to see which students may not yet have had a turn to share. Be sure to arrange opportunities for these students to participate.

6. Show the students how the Voice Bells hanging makes a sweet sound if it is gently shaken. Provide a time when students are allowed to hear their voices by shaking the hanging.

Variations

- Use the Voice Bells strategy to track other opportunities in the class, such as teacher/student conferencing, student/author read-alouds, or show and tell.

- Integrate the Voice Bells strategy into math instruction. Ask students to figure out the percentage of voices from their class that have been heard so far that day.

- Shy students can be encouraged to participate in the Voice Bells strategy as well. If a student is not ready to speak in front of the class, suggest that she whisper to the teacher or that she shake her bell to agree with someone else's comment.

Tips

☆ Metal jingle bells are often on sale at craft stores just after the Christmas holidays.

☆ Obtain bells in two colors (usually gold and silver). Place girls' names on one color, boys' on the other. This will make it easy to quickly discern if boys and girls are getting an equal opportunity to contribute.

Lightbulb Moments (3–8)

Videos and DVDs can bring almost any content to life for students. With such a wonderful assortment of relevant material available in this medium, most teachers will use video viewing as part of their instructional program. For students who are active learners, however, sitting for prolonged periods and watching a video may result in tuning out. Lightbulb Moments gives all students an opportunity to remain engaged and thinking while watching videos.

Materials

Lightbulbs (see reproducible, page 152)

Water-based, wipe-off markers

Video or DVD

How To

1. Make copies of the reproducible, laminate them, and cut out the bulbs.
2. Before viewing a video or DVD, provide each student with one or more lightbulbs and a marker.
3. Direct students to listen for Lightbulb Moments as they watch the video. Lightbulb Moments might include a strong personal connection to the content, something that amazes the student, or a revelation they have while watching.
4. When a student experiences a Lightbulb Moment, he is to write his thought on the laminated lightbulb.
5. As students view the video, remind them once or twice to listen for Lightbulb Moments.

6. At some point during the video, write and post your own Lightbulb Moments in a spot where students will notice and be reminded. This will serve as a cue to students. When the video is finished, have students post their lightbulbs on a board or wall.

7. Discuss as time permits. Ask students to share their ideas or offer connections to their peers' Lightbulb Moments.

Variation

● More-active students may benefit from posting their lightbulbs as soon as they write them. If you have students who might benefit from this, be sure to choose a posting area that will not distract other students who are viewing the video.

Detective Tools (K–5)

Reading relies heavily on our visual and auditory skills. Students who learn best in kinesthetic or tactile ways may tune out during extended reading times. Detective Tools are easy ways to add a physical interaction to any text material, thereby increasing student engagement. They also help a teacher readily observe if the student is in the right place in the text and keeping up with the class.

Materials

Plastic magnifying glasses and plastic craft eyes (flat on one side), available at toy, craft, and party supply stores

Links (often used for math manipulatives, these are usually oval but can come in shapes such as hearts and stars)

How To

1. Describe the job of a detective, and discuss some of the tools a detective might use to find things.

2. Distribute one of the objects to each student. (Allow one minute for students to play with the tools.)

3. As the students read, direct them to use their tools to find certain items. For example, you might say, "Put your eye on the noun in that sentence" or "Use your magnifying glass to find the vocabulary word."

Variations

- Rubber witches fingers (usually available in October) are fun pointing devices to be used in a similar way.

- Use mini flashlights while reading from a Big Book. Give one to a student and ask her to come up and point the light at the word with a short *e* sound, or at the comma, etc. Turn down the lights to heighten the effect!
- If students finish early, challenge them to "Be a Detective" and find any of the following items in the reading material:

  ~a word that is new to you

  ~a word that follows the "silent *e* rule"

  ~a word that describes a feeling

  ~a word that means _____

  ~a word you would like to use in your writing

  ~a word that has been on a spelling list this year

  ~a word you can tell your mother (father, sister, grandmother) about

  ~an action word

  ~a pair of words that rhyme

Cup Stacking (K–8)

One of the latest sports to come on the scene is Cup Stacking. Designed by two physical education teachers, Cup Stacking, also referred to as Speed Stacking, is an activity requiring proficient eye/hand coordination, balance, visual/spatial intelligence, and quick-thinking skills. Usually done as an individual competition, this new sport is energizing children all over the country—at recreation centers, after-school clubs, and worldwide competitions! Because of its many benefits, Cup Stacking lends itself extremely well to classroom instruction.

Materials

20-ounce, plastic-coated cups, one for each student

Water-based, wipe-off markers

How To

1. Have each student write a word or phrase on the cup. For example, if studying the food chain, each student would write one thing found in a food chain. Examples might include grass, snake, sun, frog, eagle.

2. Explain to the students that they are to stack their cups with others in the correct order of the food chain as quickly as they can. The goal is to get the tallest stack of cups in correct sequence. In our example of the food chain, the cups would be stacked, from bottom to top, as: sun, grass, frog, snake, eagle.

3. Determine the appropriate amount of time needed, and tell the students you will say "Go" when it's time to start and will blow a whistle or make some other sound to indicate they are to stop.

4. After the first round is completed, review the cup stacks with students, making sure that the cups have been placed in the correct order.

5. Have students unstack the cups and distribute them so that everyone has one. The students will not necessarily have their original cup.

6. Continue with additional rounds of Cup Stacking, encouraging students to find other ways to get taller stacks. Perhaps a student will have a cup marked "lion" and could add it near the top of a stack to make it taller.

7. When finished, simply rinse the cups with water and the marker will wash right off.

Variations

- Cup Stacking can be used to energize a wide variety of content—anything that has a correct sequence or hierarchy. Ideas include time lines, steps in a process, numerical or alphabetical order, the periodic table of elements, periods in music or art history, musical note values, or the sequence of a story.

- Provide one student with a cup that has the first step in a sequence. For example, in a lesson on the food chain, the first cup would be marked "sun." Then ask the remaining students to determine whose cup should go next. When they believe it is their turn, they should come up and place their cup on top of the most recent one.

- Cup stacking also can be used for categorizing and sorting. Instead of stacking in a linear sequence, students can make pyramids. For example, if sorting words that have short *e* sounds vs. long *e* sounds, one pyramid might have "egg," "bed," "let," "gem," "shed,"and "pen" stacked together and another pyramid might have "me," "tree," "read," "eat," "we," and "key."

Pattern Towers (K–8)

Many school concepts contain patterns. By emphasizing these patterns, teachers can assist students in grasping the concepts. Pattern Towers give students a concrete, fun way to learn things such as word families, skip counting, and rhyming words.

Materials

Plastic building blocks, such as Duplos or Legos

Water-based, wipe-off marker

How To

1. Write a word or phrase on one of the blocks with the marker. For example, if teaching word families, you might write the word *cat*.
2. Show students how to connect another block to the top of the first. Then demonstrate how to add the next word. For example, write the word *bat* on the second connecting block.
3. Instruct students to write as many words as they can think of, building the tallest tower they can.
4. When finished, simply rinse off the blocks.

Variations

- Have students build Pattern Towers with numbers—emphasize skip counting, prime numbers, multiples, even or odd numbers, etc.
- Plastic blocks can be used for abstract concepts, such as elements of a community. Have students write a characteristic of an ideal community on each block, then build a community with the blocks. For example, students

might write terms such as *respectful, diverse, justice, creative, peace,* etc., and show, through their block structure, how these characteristics connect or build upon each other.

Tips

☆ If you have wooden blocks instead of plastic, cover them with plain contact paper. Students can use water-based markers on the contact paper and then wipe it off with a damp tissue.

☆ Consider having students work in pairs to support each other's learning.

Twist and Spell (K–5)

Spelling practice can be a chore for many students. Strategies that turn spelling practice into fun, while also strengthening the learning process, are a plus for any classroom. Twist and Spell, originally designed as a spelling activity, can be adapted to enhance math facts practice, too!

Materials

Styrofoam coffee cups with a wide lip
Black marker and bold, colored marker

How To

1. Using a black and a colored marker, write the letters of the alphabet around the rim of an upside-down Styrofoam cup. Mark the consonants in black and the vowels in color, and space the letters evenly around the cup (see illustration).

2. Continue to mark cups in this fashion until you have enough for Twist and Spell. One student will require 6 to 10 cups; a small group, 30 cups.

3. Mark one cup with an arrow (see illustration).

4. Choose a spelling word to demonstrate Twist and Spell to the students. For example, if the word is *child*, you will need five cups, one for each letter.

5. Stack the cups upside down and place the arrow cup so that the arrow is pointing at the letters below.

6. Twist the arrow cup until it is pointing at the first letter in the word (for example, *c* for the word *child*).

7. Twist the second cup until the second letter (*h*) of the word lines up under the first letter. Continue twisting each successive cup until the correct letters for the word (*child*) are lined up under the arrow.

Variation

- Twist and Spell cups can be designed to use for practicing math facts. Instead of letters, mark the numerals 0 through 9 around the cup, adding +, −, ×, ÷, and = at the end. The operational signs should be in a contrasting color.

Tip

☆ To space your letters evenly, mark *a* first, then mark *m* and *n* on the opposite side. The letter *g* will go halfway between *a* and *m*, and the letter *t* will go just shy of halfway between *n* and *a*. Then fill in the remaining letters.

Spelling Keyboard (K–8)

Scientists have found that language and music are closely linked in the brain, even sharing some of the same neural circuits. By combining music with semantic learning, we can increase our ability to retain information. The Spelling Keyboard strategy does just that! It provides a way for students to associate specific musical input with the accurate spelling of words.

Materials

Small, musical keyboard (usually under $10)

Small sticky dots or labels that will fit on the keys

How To

1. On each sticky dot, write a letter of the alphabet, using a different color of ink or a different-colored dot for vowels.

2. Stick the dots on the keys in alphabetical order, placing the vowels on the black keys and the consonants on the white keys (see illustration).

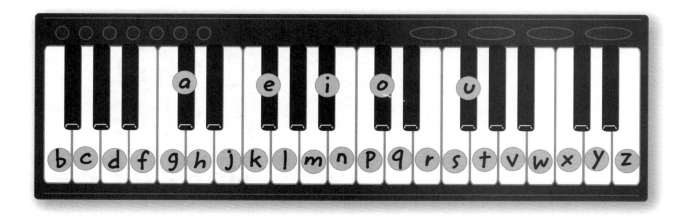

3. Give a student a word to spell and direct him to press the corresponding keys on the keyboard as he says the letters aloud. Repeat at least two more times.

4. If working with a group, ask several children to play the same word before moving on to the next word on the list. Each word will have its own unique tune so that students can sing along!

Variations

- Not teaching spelling? A keyboard can be used to enhance other learning, too. Obtain three or four keyboards. Write the letters A, B, C, and D on sticky dots. Place the A dot on the lowest white key, the B dot about one-third of the way up the keyboard, the C dot two-thirds of the way up the keyboard, and the D dot on the highest white key. Put students into cooperative groups, each group with its own keyboard. Pose multiple-choice questions to the class, allowing several seconds for the group to confer about the answer. When you call time, students must press the corresponding key to the correct answer.

- To add even greater tactile input, write the letters with colored puff paint (found at most craft stores).

Tips

☆ For center work, it is helpful to have keyboards that allow plug-in headphones.

☆ When using multiple keyboards for cooperative groups (see Variations above), be sure to place the A, B, C, and D dots on the same keys on each keyboard. That way it will be easy to hear if students are all in agreement or in disagreement.

[Adapted from Beninghof, A. (2003) *Meeting Standards: Instructional strategies for struggling students*. Longmont, CO: Sopris West.]

Tennis Spelling (K–6)

Interdisciplinary lessons connect two or more content areas simultaneously, providing students with a more integrated experience. Physical education classes are a wonderful place to introduce interdisciplinary lessons, as they naturally provide for the kinesthetic opportunities many students need. Tennis Spelling, developed by a P.E. teacher, is a fun, physical approach to spelling practice.

Materials

Large supply of tennis or plastic balls (the number will vary, depending on the number of relay teams, but start with about 100)

Permanent marker

How To

1. With a permanent marker, write a letter of the alphabet on each ball. Be sure that each letter is represented at least twice, with the most commonly used letters (*aeiouwrtypdghlcbnm*) represented four or more times.
2. Place all the balls on the floor along one end of the gymnasium.
3. At the opposite end of the gym, direct students to line up in two relay teams. (Three or more teams can be assigned if you have a larger number of balls.)
4. Explain to the students that they will be spelling words as a relay team. You will call out a spelling word, and when you say "Go," the first student in line on both teams runs to the opposite side of the gym and finds the first letter of the word. They pick it up and bring it back to their team, laying it on the floor nearby. As soon as they have put the ball down, the second

student in the line runs down and gets the second letter in the word. They continue in this fashion until the word is completely spelled.

5. After both teams have completed the word, check the spelling. Each team that spells the word correctly receives 50 points. The team that finishes first and spells the word correctly receives 60 points.

6. Roll the balls back to the opposite side of the gym before announcing the next word.

Variations

- At a prespelling level, use the alphabet balls to play an alphabet relay. Have each relay team line up the balls in alphabetical order, A through Z.
- Mark the balls with numbers instead of letters and do Tennis Math. Call out a math problem with a two- or three-digit answer. Each student runs and grabs one of the numerals in the answer.
- At a precomputation level, use the number balls to play a number relay. Have each relay team line up the balls in numerical order, 1 through 20.
- If balls are not available, the letters or numbers can be placed on pieces of paper, envelopes, empty milk cartons, plastic Easter eggs, or almost any other small object.

Tips

☆ Ask a local tennis or golf facility to donate used balls.

☆ Place a thin piece of foam, approximately 2 x 3 feet, on the floor next to each relay team. Direct the students to place the balls on the foam as they spell the word. This will keep the balls from rolling away.

☆ Carefully consider whether you will allow team members to help each other with the task. If you want each student to be responsible for spelling the words accurately, direct the students to remain quiet during the relay.

☆ Be sure to place struggling spellers in a relay spot in which they will experience success. For example, the first letter of a word is often the easiest to determine.

Brain Bags (K–8)

Brain research tells us that when students use multiple modalities in their learning, their recall of the information will be more accurate (Jensen, 1997). Brain Bags were designed with this research in mind. These simple bags can be used to stimulate ideas and learning in a wide variety of content areas and for students of many ages. Plus, the conceptual imagery encourages students to believe that they have the necessary knowledge for the assignment—they just need to "shake their brains" a bit.

Materials

Pictures of brains

Brown paper lunch bag for each student

How To

1. Show students pictures of brains. Point out the physical characteristics, such as the color and the wrinkled texture.
2. Explain to students that they will each be making a brain, and provide each with a brown paper lunch bag.
3. Direct students to label their bags with their names, such as "Matt's Brain," and then show them how to open their bags and wrinkle them (without popping them!).
4. Once students have made their Brain Bags, information can be placed inside them. For example, in a writing lesson, a teacher may want to focus on students' abilities to generate new, creative ideas. Brain Bags are a wonderful tool for this purpose. Provide the students with slips of paper that have the names of common household objects. After the students

have placed these into their bags, direct them to close the bags and "shake their brains." After a few moments of shaking, direct the students to pull out two of the slips of paper, identifying two common objects. With these objects in mind, they are to write a paragraph describing a new invention that combines the two objects.

Variations

- Use Brain Bags for math by filling them with slips of paper containing single-digit numbers. Students can pull out two or more numbers and make up word problems or math facts.
- Brain Bags can be used to store rich vocabulary words that students generate in class. Often, teachers will call these "Wow" words and might have students keep lists of them on bulletin boards or in journals. Instead, have students write them on slips of paper and place them into their bags. During a writing assignment, encourage students to "shake their brains" and pull out two or three words to spice up their writing.

MATT'S BRAIN

Colorful Speech (2–8)

Every school-age child is taught that our language is made up of "parts of speech." There are specific rules governing the use of various parts of speech in verbal and written communication. While many students grasp this concept quickly, others find the whole notion to be too abstract. Colorful Speech is an approach to teaching parts of speech that makes the concept more concrete and understandable.

Materials

Colorful Speech sheets (see reproducible, page 153)

Unifix cubes, or other connecting blocks of various colors (Unifix cubes are generally used as math manipulatives and are often available in primary-school classrooms.)

How To

1. Distribute a Colorful Speech sheet and a set of colored cubes to each student.
2. Referring to the Colorful Speech sheet, write the color key on the board.
3. Explain to the students that each word in a sentence is a different part of speech, as they have been studying. Direct them to the color key on the board, pointing out that each part of speech has been assigned a color.
4. Write a sentence on the board, such as follows, and assign the appropriate color to each word, getting help from the students.

The	cat	ran	into	the	street.
Black	Blue	Red	Yellow	Black	Blue

5. Direct students to look at their Colorful Speech sheet and choose a colored cube for each word in sentence #1 based on the color key on their sheet. Then have them build their sentences by connecting their cubes.

6. Allow time for students to practice with sentences #2 – #4.

Variations

- Using a water-based marker, write the parts of speech on the corresponding colored cubes. This will eliminate the need for students to refer to a separate key.

- Simplify the activity for students by having them work on fewer parts of speech, for example nouns and verbs. Adapt the activity for students who are ready for greater complexity by adding higher concepts such as proper nouns.

- If students have not yet been introduced to all the parts of speech, design the lesson and the color key to include only those parts taught.

- Use Colorful Speech cubes as a way to enhance editing skills. Direct students to review their writing and make sure that every sentence contains a blue and red cube (noun and verb).

- After students show consistent success using the Colorful Speech cubes, transition them to using crayons or colored pencils to draw boxes around the words in their sentences.

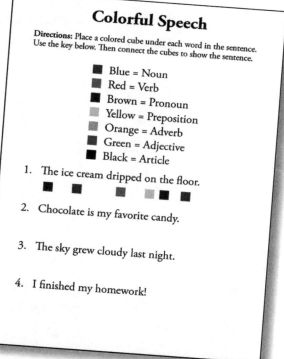

Colorful Speech

Directions: Place a colored cube under each word in the sentence. Use the key below. Then connect the cubes to show the sentence.

- Blue = Noun
- Red = Verb
- Brown = Pronoun
- Yellow = Preposition
- Orange = Adverb
- Green = Adjective
- Black = Article

1. The ice cream dripped on the floor.
2. Chocolate is my favorite candy.
3. The sky grew cloudy last night.
4. I finished my homework!

Spelling Bells (K–5)

The reading wars of the last decade have pitted whole-language advocates against phonics proponents in heated debate over which approach is best for students. But there are some common beliefs between these two groups—one of which is the need for students to practice spelling words. Repetitive practice can increase retention, but only if students are engaged and activating their memory paths. Spelling Bells is a practice technique that turns spelling into a multimodality event, thereby strengthening memory.

Materials

26 metal jingle bells

Permanent black marker

Two-foot piece of yarn or string

Large-eyed needle

How To

1. Write the letters of the alphabet on the sides of the jingle bells, using the marker. (Jingle bells have four sides; write the same letter on each of the four sides.)

2. Thread the yarn through the needle, string the bells onto the yarn in alphabetical order, and tie a knot between each bell so that they will not slide (see illustration).

3. Attach both ends of the string of Spelling Bells onto a wall or a bulletin board. They should be hung horizontally at a height that can be reached by students.

4. During center or independent study time, direct students to go to the Spelling Bells to practice their spelling words. They are to look at a word from their list and then tap the corresponding bells in correct order to spell the word. As they tap each bell, there will be a soft jingle sound.

Variations

- Sew each bell, in order, onto a strip of heavy fabric. Staple the fabric to the board or wall.

- Spelling Bells can also be used with students who are not yet ready to learn spelling. Ask the student to touch each of the bells in order and say the letter name.

Tips

☆ Make several strings of Spelling Bells so that more than one student can practice at a time.

☆ Jingle bells are often on sale in early January.

☆ Spelling Bells are a musical way to work on alphabetizing skills. Instead of just writing the words on paper, students have to seek out the letters. The more they do this, the faster their knowledge develops of correct alphabetical order.

Board Relay   (K–8)

When someone sits for 20 minutes or more, blood begins to pool in the lower half of the body. Within seconds of standing up, the blood flow to the brain is increased by 15 percent. In other words, if students have been sitting in a classroom for more than 20 minutes, the blood in the brain has decreased by 15 percent! Board Relay reverses this by getting students up and moving in a fun, fast-paced instructional experience. As an added bonus, Board Relay does not require any advance preparation or purchasing on the part of the teacher.

How To

1. Divide the class into four relay teams. Team membership should be heterogeneous.

2. Review the rules of Board Relay with the students:
   - No running.
   - No shouting out answers.
   - If using dry-erase markers, caps must be replaced after each turn.
   - Marker or chalk must be placed on the ledge after each turn.
   - Winners will be determined based on accuracy as well as speed.

3. Divide the board into four sections and place chalk or a marker on the ledge beneath each section.

4. Determine the task for Board Relay. For example, students might be required to list 10 examples of the concept just taught, compose a sentence using an assigned vocabulary word, skip count by 5s to 50, etc.

5. Explain to students that they will each take a turn in completing the task, as in a relay. Depending on the assignment, clarify for students how much should be done in each turn. For example, in skip counting by 5s, each

student would list the next number in the sequence. Students will most likely have multiple turns before the round is over.

6. Explain that finish times will be kept for each team, but that finishing first does not mean winning—accuracy is more important.

7. Determine and convey a scoring system. For example, finishing first is worth 100 points, second is 90 points, third is 80 points, and fourth is 70 points. But for every error, the team loses 15 points.

8. Start the Board Relay. As necessary, remind students of the rules.

9. Mark the finishing order of each team on the board. When the last team has completed the task, engage the whole group in reviewing the work of each team for accuracy.

10. Note total scores for each team and repeat with a new task.

Variations

- Board Relays can be done in partners, so that no student is left on his own to complete a step of the task. Partners should be assigned by the teacher with the purpose of pairing a more-able student with a student in need of support.

- If boards are not available, place four sheets of chart paper on the wall, one per team.

- Seated Relay is a variation that reduces the physical movement in the room. For Seated Relay you will need one small whiteboard and marker per team. The student in the first position of the relay writes on the whiteboard while seated at her desk, and then passes it back to the next student.

Tip

☆ Be thoughtful of the relay positions assigned to students. If one step of the assigned task is likely to be the most difficult, assign that relay position to a student who is more ready for the challenge. Or, if one step of the task might be less complex than others, assign a student who is currently functioning at that level to that relay position.

Pass the Plate (K–6)

Developing students who are able to think "out of the box" is a goal of many teachers. Pass the Plate is a high-energy activity that encourages students to generate a wide variety of ideas and exposes all students to creative thinking. Pass the Plate (Peterson, 2004) also allows students who are English language learners to be exposed to a wealth of rich vocabulary words.

Materials

6 plastic disposable plates
Water-based, wipe-off markers

How To

1. Place students in heterogeneous groups and provide each group with a plate and a marker.

2. Explain to the students that you will announce a word. One of the group members is to write the word in the center of the plate. For example, the word might be *big*.

3. Once the word has been written, tell the students that they will have two minutes to generate as many synonyms for the word as possible. Each student is to take a turn and write a synonym on the plate around the edge. The plate is to be passed around the group as quickly as possible. If a student cannot think of a word, he can pass.

4. Explain that each word will generate points but that the most points will be awarded to words that are not found on any other plate.

5. If necessary, provide examples, such as *large* or *gigantic*, and more-creative examples, such as *gargantuan* and *supersized*.

6. After the time period is finished, help students in determining their points. Award 10 points for each word on the plate, and 50 points for any word that no other group has written.

7. When finished, simply rinse the plates off and store for another time.

Variation

- Pass the Plate can be used to generate creative examples in a wide variety of content areas. Students can list examples of verbs, mammals, carbohydrates, science fiction titles, prime numbers, artists, etc.

Tip

☆ If there is a student who might struggle with this activity, carefully consider which position might be best for her. For example, going first or second is usually easier than fifth or sixth.

TP the Room (1–8)

Children are intrigued by events with a hint of mischief behind them. When teachers capitalize on this interest, student engagement is increased. This instructional technique builds on a common neighborhood event—rolling a house with toilet paper. This usually happens secretly, in the dead of night, instead of in the classroom, but it can easily be turned into a more positive, explicit experience.

Materials

Rolls of toilet paper

Felt-tipped markers

How To

1. Assign students to heterogeneous groups, keeping the size at fewer than five, if possible, and provide each group with a roll of toilet paper and a felt-tipped marker.

2. Ask the students if they have ever seen someone's house that has been TP'd or rolled. Explain that they will have the chance to TP their classroom at the end of the activity.

3. Choose an area of the content in which you want students to be able to provide multiple examples of a concept. Depending on the grade level, students might be expected to provide a variety of examples of nouns, words with a short *a* sound, numbers that are multiples of 3, and so forth.

4. Tell the students that you will give them a signal to start and to stop. When the start signal occurs, they are to work together to generate as many examples as possible, writing each one on a piece of toilet paper, without detach-

ing it from the other pieces. The goal is to come up with as many correct examples as possible, because they will be allowed to TP the classroom with as much toilet paper as they have generated.

5. Allow students sufficient time, depending on the task and your observations.

6. After you give the stop signal, engage students in sharing some examples. Then let them drape the toilet paper around the room.

Variations

- This can also be done as a whole-class activity, with every student expected to contribute at least one example to the list.

- Consider ways to raise the level of challenge for students who are ready. For example, if they were listing examples of verbs, these students could be encouraged to contribute irregular verbs.

Tips

☆ Hotels and other public establishments often dispose of toilet paper rolls once they have reached about quarter size. Check to see if you can get some rolls donated for your class.

☆ Give the school custodian some advance warning of this activity, so that he or she understands that you will clean up the "mess."

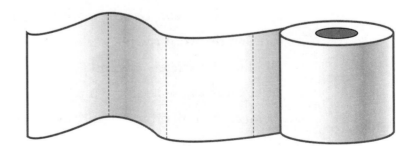

Stretch 'ems (K–5)

Phonemic awareness, a person's ability to recognize and manipulate individual sounds in a word, is essential to fluent reading. Many literacy programs are teaching students to "stretch out" the words as they attempt to decode or encode. Stretch 'ems make this approach even more effective by giving students a concrete, stretchy medium.

Materials

Card stock

⅛-inch-wide sewing elastic (found anywhere sewing supplies are sold)

Water-based, wipe-off markers

How To

1. Cut the card stock into 1½ x 2½-inch rectangles and laminate the cards.

2. Using scissors, make two small slits at the top (one of the short ends) of each card.

3. Thread the elastic through the slits, stringing three, four, five, or more cards together so that they lie flat, side by side. Tie a knot in each end of the elastic.

4. Choose a word that is appropriate for your class, like *peanut*, and select a 5-card Stretch 'em. Use the marker to write one or two letters on each card, forming the word *peanut*.

5. Hold up the Stretch 'em and gently pull on both ends of the elastic. The letter cards will separate, resulting in a stretching out of the word. The stronger the pull on the elastic, the greater the separation (see illustration).

6. Draw students' attention to how the letters sound individually. Then slowly reduce the tension on the elastic, bringing the letters closer together, verbally blending them to form the word.

7. Provide each student with a Stretch 'em and a marker and allow them to experiment.

Variations

- For more-advanced students, use Stretch 'ems to work on syllabication skills. Have the student break a multisyllabic word into separate syllables, writing one syllable on each card. The student might also work as a peer tutor, showing another student how words can be broken up into separate syllables, stretching the Stretch 'em to demonstrate.

- Flip up a letter and ask a student how the word will sound with the change.

- Use Stretch 'ems to practice math facts, leaving the answer flipped up.

- Use Stretch 'ems to follow a multistep process, using one card for each step. For example, if teaching a four-step problem-solving process, the first card might read "Describe Problem," followed by "Determine Objective," "Brainstorm Solutions," and "Make Choices."

Tips

☆ Make sure the slits at the top of the card are small enough to grab at the elastic. If they are too big, the cards will slide around too much.

☆ Keep a supply of Stretch 'ems at writing centers or in your book corner so that students can independently access them.

Vocabulary Stack (2–6)

The more often a student uses a new vocabulary word in meaningful context, the more likely he will retain it. While textbooks often use new vocabulary several times in a chapter, the student may not generalize the word beyond the text. Vocabulary Stack motivates students to create opportunities to use new words meaningfully and frequently.

Materials
Poster board

Pennies

How To

1. Draw a grid on the poster board (see illustration) and label it Vocabulary Stack.

2. Write the names of the students in the class down the left-hand column, and write the new vocabulary words for the unit or chapter across the top.

3. Lay the poster flat in an accessible spot but one that isn't likely to get bumped.

4. Tell the students that every time they use one of the new vocabulary words in a meaningful context, they will receive a penny to place on the grid. Demonstrate how to place the penny in the space at the intersection of a student's name and a word.

5. With student help, identify a purchase that will be made with the pennies, for example popcorn or a new book for the classroom.

6. On occasion, draw attention to the Vocabulary Stack. Discuss its three-dimensional aspects. Ask students to draw conclusions based on what they see.

Variation

- Vocabulary Stack can be used to motivate students to use new vocabulary in their written work. Every time a student demonstrates the correct usage of a word in her journal, allow her to place a penny on the grid.

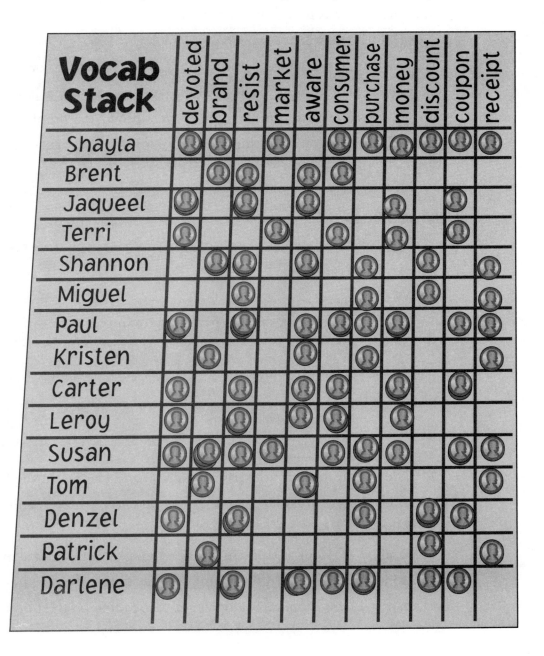

Vocab Stack	devoted	brand	resist	market	aware	consumer	purchase	money	discount	coupon	receipt
Shayla	●	●		●		●	●	●	●	●	●
Brent		●	●		●	●					
Jaqueel	●		●		●		●		●		
Terri	●			●		●		●		●	
Shannon		●	●		●		●		●		●
Miguel			●				●		●		●
Paul	●		●		●	●	●	●		●	●
Kristen		●			●		●				●
Carter	●		●		●	●		●		●	
Leroy	●		●		●	●		●			
Susan	●	●	●	●		●	●	●		●	●
Tom		●			●			●			●
Denzel	●		●				●		●	●	
Patrick		●							●		●
Darlene	●		●		●	●	●		●	●	

Stepping Stones (K-8)

Brain research has found that novel input makes the brain allocate nerve cells and stimulate neuronal connections (Jensen, E., 1997). This is good for kids! The challenge for teachers is to find ways to add novelty to our teaching. One method for achieving this is by catching students' attention in an unusual way as they enter the classroom. Stepping Stones provides a simple way to catch attention, add novelty, and stimulate thinking about the curriculum before class even begins.

Materials

Clear-plastic page protectors (available where office supplies are sold)

How To

1. Write a prompt on a sheet of paper. For example:

   2 + 2 = _____.

   The capital of Colorado is _____.

   Brutus is a _____.

   Noun _____

   1.07 _____

2. Slide the prompt into the page protector, and place it on the floor outside the classroom. You may choose to line up two or three in a row as Stepping Stones, creating a path into the classroom.

3. Stand by the door as students are arriving. Direct them to step on the "stone" and respond to the prompt. For example, they might provide the answer, a definition, an example, etc., depending on the prompt.

Variations

- For older students, there is no need to direct them to step on the "stone." As they approach the room, their attention will be drawn to it, and it will activate their thinking about the content.

- Make copies of a handprint (see reproducible, page 154), cut them out, and laminate them. Using a water-based, wipe-off marker, write a prompt on each hand. Stick the hands around the top of the door frame. As students enter the room, allow them to jump up and hit a hand, responding to the prompt as they do so.

- Place one or more Stepping Stones on the floor outside the classroom door. As students exit the room, they must step on each and tell you their answers.

Tip

☆ If the floor is carpeted, consider applying some bits of adhesive-backed, hooked Velcro to the back corners of the sheet protector. This will help the "stones" to stay in place.

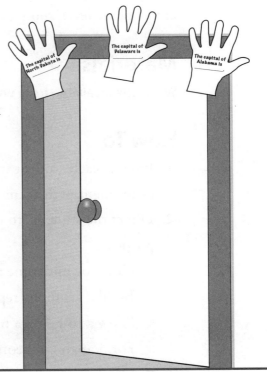

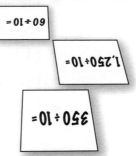

Wikki Stix (K–8)

One of the most versatile materials a teacher can have on hand is a set of Wikki Stix. Wikki Stix are strings covered in wax. Like pipe cleaners, they can be used to form shapes, letters, and numbers, but are a safer material because they do not have a metal center. Wikki Stix can be used to make any content, at any grade level, more interactive and engaging.

Materials

Wikki Stix (available from **www.crystalsprings.com** and from **www.wikkistix.com**)

How To

1. Provide each student with one or more Wikki Stix, and allow students to experiment with them for a few minutes.

2. Direct the students to use their Wikki Stix for any of the following purposes:

   ■ Circle or underline an important point in the text.

   ■ Build a symbolic representation of their learning.

   ■ Show a route on a map or globe.

   ■ Form angles or geometric shapes.

   ■ Design a graphic organizer, such as a Venn diagram.

   ■ Divide their paper into pros and cons.

   ■ Make line graphs.

   ■ Practice spelling words by forming letters with the Wikki Stix.

   ■ Create atoms, molecules, or models.

Variation

- If a permanent product is desired, students can do a "rubbing" over the Wikki Stix. For example, to record spelling words, direct students to place a sheet of paper on top of the Wikki Stix and use the side of a crayon to rub color over the page. The shape of the Wikki Stix will be darker on the paper than the rest of the page.

Tip

☆ Store Wikki Stix in sets of five in small, resealable plastic bags. Use a permanent marker to write the number 5 on the outside of the bag. As you distribute the bags to students, explain that there are five in each bag, and there must be five when returned at the end of the lesson. This will ensure that your supply lasts for the entire year!

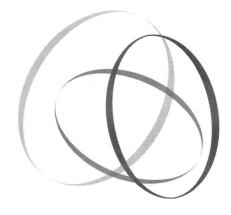

References

Beninghof, A. (1993) *Ideas for inclusion: The classroom teacher's guide.* Longmont, CO: Sopris West.

Beninghof, A. (1998) *SenseAble strategies: Including diverse learners through multisensory strategies.* Longmont, CO: Sopris West.

Beninghof, A. (2003) *Meeting Standards: Instructional strategies for struggling students.* Longmont, CO: Sopris West.

Dunn, R. (1988) Commentary: Teaching students through their perceptual strengths or preferences. *Journal of Reading* 31, (4), 304–309.

Dunn, R. & Dunn, K. (1993) *Teaching secondary students through their individual learning styles: Practical approaches for grades 7–12.* Boston: Allyn & Bacon.

Individuals with Disabilities Education Improvement Act of 2004 (IDEA), P. L. 108–446, 118 Stat. 2647.

Jensen, E. (1997) *Brain compatible strategies.* Del Mar, CA: Turning Point Publishing.

Kulik, J. A. (1992) *An analysis of the research on ability grouping: Historical and contemporary perspectives* (RBDM 9204). Storrs, CT: The National Research Center on the Gifted and Talented, University of Connecticut.

Marzano, R., Pickering, D. & Pollock, J. (2001) *Classroom instruction that works: Research-based strategies for increasing student achievement.* Alexandria, VA: ASCD.

Mohrmann, S. (1990) *Reading styles progress report.* Syosset, NY: National Reading Styles Institute.

Peterson, M. (2004) *Accelerating the literacy development and academic performance of your ESL students.* Bureau of Education and Research: Belleview, WA.

Sinnot, S. (1999) *Welcome to Kirsten's world.* Pleasant Company: Middleton, WI.

Sprenger, M. (1999) *Learning and memory: The brain in action.* Alexandria, VA: ASCD.

Thompson, A. L. (2003) *Inspection for inclusion: Monitoring for responsible inclusion of children with disabilities in general education,* a paper for the Together to School Again Conference, Utrecht, The Netherlands.

Tomlinson, C. (1999) *The differentiated classroom: Responding to the needs of all learners.* Alexandria, VA: ASCD.

Yong, R. & McIntyre, J. (1992) A comparative study of the learning style preferences of students with learning disabilities and students who are gifted. *Journal of Learning Disabilities,* 25, (2), 124–132.

Challenge Questions for Literacy

What are some of the things you wondered about while this was happening?

Pick one vocabulary word. What short rhyme can you make up that includes the word?

How is this story different from a story you read last week?

How does this story compare to life in your house?

What would your mother think of this story?

What do you think is the most important idea in this story? Defend your choice.

If you were the main character in this story, what would you have done?

How might this story be written if it were to take place 200 years in the future?

How many ways can you think of to solve one of the problems in this story? Describe each one.

What could you change in this story that would affect the outcome?

Does this story remind you of any fairy tales or fables?

Would this story make a good movie? Why or why not?

Challenge Questions for History

What are some of the things you wondered about while you were reading?

Pick one vocabulary word. What do you think its historical origin is?

How does this time period in history differ from the last one we studied?

How does this historical experience compare to a time in your own life?

What would your mother (father, grandparent) say about this event in history?

What do you think was the most important single action during this period? Prepare to defend your choice.

If you were a leader during this time period, what would you have done?

How might this event be different if it were to take place 200 years in the future?

Pick a person who is currently famous. How would he or she have handled this problem in history?

What could you change in this story that would affect the outcome?

Does this period in time remind you of any others?

What type of movie would you make about this time in history? Describe it.

Challenge Questions for Mathematics

What were some of the things you wondered about while doing this lesson?

If you were teaching this math concept to someone, how would you teach it in a different way?

How might your mother (father, grandparent) apply this math concept to her life?

If you were writing a fictional story that involved this math concept, what would the title of the story be?

Does this math concept remind you of any others we've studied this year? How?

What rhyme or rap can you develop to help someone remember this math concept?

Where might you find examples of this math concept in nature?

What could you invent that would require this math concept?

How might this math concept apply to a household appliance? Explain.

If you had to apply a color to this math concept, what would it be? Why?

How was this math concept utilized in some way in a movie you have seen or heard about?

How might people in another country view this math concept differently?

Challenge Questions for Science

Pick a person who is currently famous. How does this science concept relate to his or her life?

If you were teaching this science concept to someone, how would you teach it in a different way?

How might your mother (father, grandparent) apply this science concept to her life?

If you were writing a fictional story that involved this science concept, what would the title of the story be?

Does this science concept remind you of any others we've studied this year? How?

What rhyme or rap can you develop to help someone remember this science concept?

What prediction can you make about how this science concept will advance in 500 years?

What could you invent that would require this science concept?

How could you make money from your understanding of this science concept?

What might happen if you reversed this process?

How was this science concept used in some way in a movie you have seen or heard about?

How might geography affect this science concept?

Homework Review Data Sheet

Directions: During homework review, keep track of:

- ☐ The number of boys who raised their hands and the number of girls who raised their hands
- ☐ The number of times students on the left side of the room were called on vs. that of the right side of the room
- ☐ The number of times students in the front of the room were called on vs. that of the back of the room
- ☐ The number of times a real-world connection was mentioned by girls vs. that by boys
- ☐ The number of questions that were asked by students
- ☐ The number of questions that were asked by the teacher

Collect your data here.

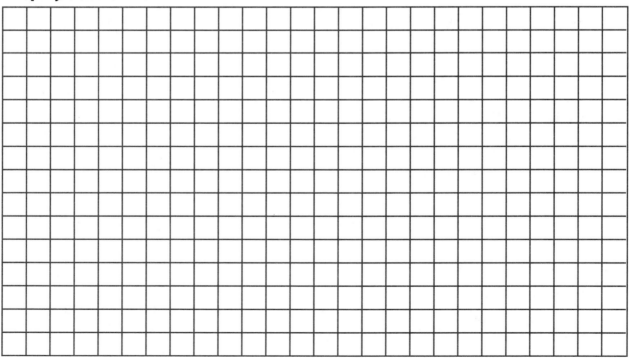

Graph your data here.

Reading Task Card

First:

Then pick one of these:

 Make up test questions, with answers, about the story. Give them to the teacher.

 Write a story that is connected to what you read.

 Build something that shows what you learned from your reading. Use blocks, paper, or other things you can find in the room.

Draw a picture of something from your book.

 Make up a game using the theme of your book. Make up rules and directions. Play it with a friend.

 Write a song about the story you read. Sing it to a friend.

Reading Task Card

Name: _____ **Date:** _____

Must Do...

- ☐ Before reading, randomly place six sticky notes in your book. When you encounter a sticky as you read, write a question on it related to what you just read.

- ☐ Draw three pictures that show the conclusion of the story.

- ☐ Create a poem about the story.

When finished, do as many of these as possible...

- ☐ Using the computer, find out about the author of the story.

- ☐ Write a dialogue between two characters about why you don't want to do something that someone else wants you to do. Act it out with a friend.

- ☐ Build a vocabulary tower, writing on Legos the singular and plural nouns you can find in the story.

- ☐ Write a diary entry as if you were a character from the story. Decorate it with period artwork.

- ☐ Make three to five riddles about the story or similar ideas.

Math Task Card

First:

Then pick one of these:

 Make up test questions, with answers, about the math lesson. Give them to the teacher.

 Write a math story that includes what you learned in math today.

Build something that shows what you learned in math today. Use blocks, paper, or other things you can find in the room.

 Make a treasure hunt for something in the room. Make up clues that use math. Have a friend follow the clues.

 Draw a picture. Use the math you learned today. Label the drawing using math.

 Make up a game that uses the math you learned today. Make up rules and directions. Play it with a friend.

 Write a song about the math you learned today. Sing it to a friend.

Math Task Card

Name: _____ **Date:** _____

Must Do...

    Do number _____ on page _____

    Do number _____ on page _____

_____

When finished, do as many of these as possible...

    ☐ Make up two sample test questions, with answers, that relate to this math lesson. Hand them in to the teacher.

    ☐ Write a math story (fiction) that includes the concepts presented in this lesson.

    ☐ Build something out of Legos, paper, or whatever materials you can find, using the math concepts from this lesson. Explain your thinking below.

    ☐ _____

           _____

    ☐ Develop a treasure hunt for something that exists in this classroom. Make up clues that use the math learned in this lesson. Have a friend follow the clues.

    ☐ Draw something based on the concepts presented in this lesson. Label the drawing with explanations of the math you used.

    ☐ Make up a game that includes math concepts. Develop rules and directions. Play it with a friend.

Math Task Card

Name: _____ **Date:** _____

Must Do...

    Do number _____ on page _____

    Do number _____ on page _____

    _____

When finished, do as many of these as possible...

☐ Make up a shopping trip to the mall. Use the concepts presented in the lesson.

☐ Write a rap song that includes the math from this lesson.

☐ Write up questions about the math lesson, and ask someone in the class to answer them. Write down his or her answers.

☐ Write a paragraph about how you felt about the math concepts from this lesson. Were they easy? Hard? How did you figure them out?

☐ Draw a book cover for a math book based on this lesson. Be sure to include a title and illustrations that include the specific topic of the lesson.

☐ Make up a card game that includes the concepts from the lesson. The concepts might be used in the process of playing or in the rules for scoring. Play it with a friend.

Challenge Authority Cards

Listen for a point that the teacher makes that you think you could debate. Debate the teacher, using supportive examples or evidence to prove your point.

Prepare a false answer to one of the questions, and try to convince the teacher or students that you are correct.

Question the text. Did the textbook authors make any errors? Use any poor examples? Have a biased perspective? Leave out something essential?

How could you "fix" this experiment/game/situation (i.e., cheat) so that the outcome would be different?

Look for cultural bias in the lesson. Would other cultures view it the same way? Make the same choices?

Pick a Path

Personal Meter

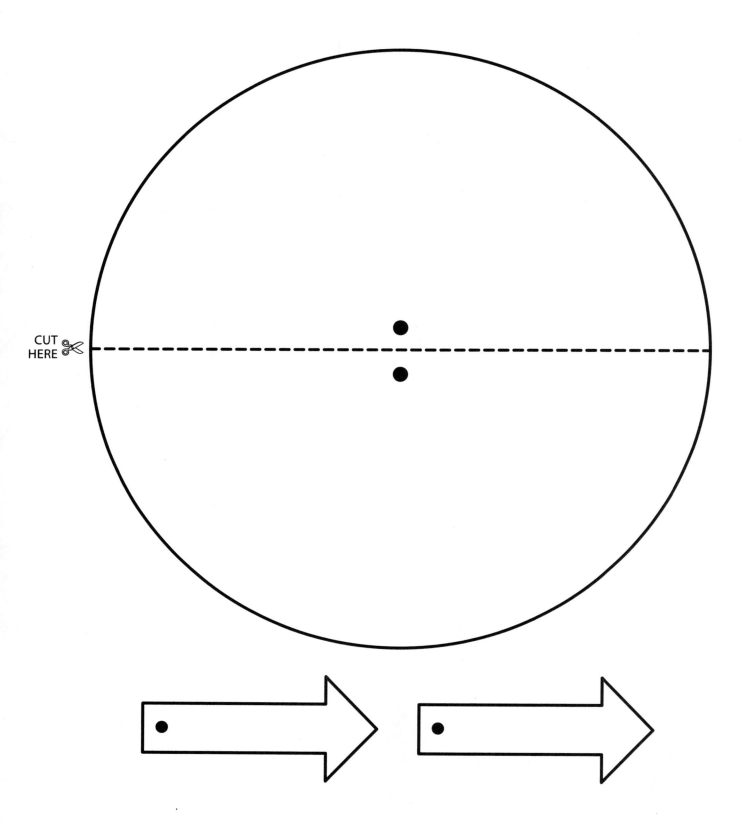

CUT
HERE

Strongly Agree

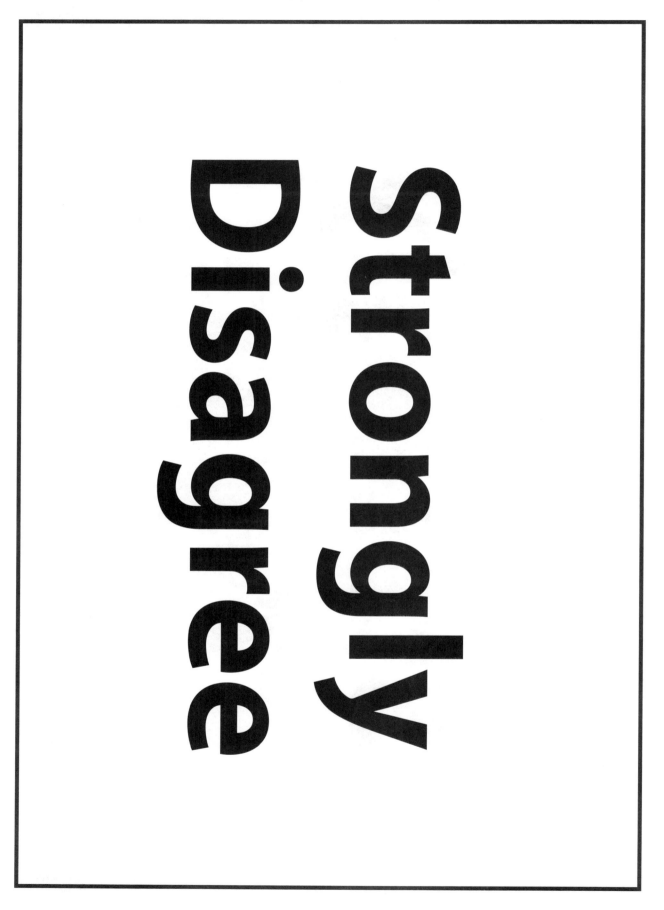

Strongly Disagree

_____'s Ticket out the Door

_____'s Ticket out the Door

_____'s Ticket out the Door

_____'s Ticket out the Door

_____'s Ticket out the Door

Text Retell Cards

As we are reading, think about how you might teach this information to a **5-year-old child**.

Be prepared, when I call on you, to reword the most recent part of what we read.

Remember, pretend you are telling it to a **5-year-old child**.

As we are reading, think about how you might teach this information to a **95-year-old grandparent** who has never had this class.

Be prepared, when I call on you, to reword the most recent part of what we read.

Remember, pretend you are telling it to a **95-year-old grandparent** who has never had this class.

As we are reading, think about how you might teach this information if you were a **cartoon character** from television (Bart Simpson, Spider-Man, SpongeBob, etc.).

Be prepared, when I call on you, to reword the most recent part of what we read.

Remember, pretend you are a **cartoon character.**

Direction Retell Cards

Pick any **cartoon character** from television or the movies. Retell the directions as if you were that character.

Pretend you are giving the directions to a **5-year-old child.** Retell the directions.

Think of a **famous person.** Retell the directions as if you were that person.

Pick out the **main words** in the directions and repeat them in the correct order.

Pretend you are giving the directions to a **95-year-old person.** Retell the directions.

Retell the directions in **a rap or a rhyme.**

Graphic Organizer Puzzle Shapes

Boomerang Bookmarks

Name _____

Directions:
Write a question for _____ of the question words below.

Who

What

When

Where

Why

How

Name _____

Directions:
Write a question for _____ of the question words below.

Who

What

When

Where

Why

How

Boomerang Bookmarks

Name _____

Directions:
Answer _____ of the
questions below.

Who is it about?

What happened?

When did it happen?

Where is the story taking place?

Why did it happen?

How did the character feel?

Name _____

Directions:
Answer _____ of the
questions below.

Who is it about?

What happened?

When did it happen?

Where is the story taking place?

Why did it happen?

How did the character feel?

Boomerang Bookmarks

Name _____	**Name** _____
Directions: Answer _____ of the questions below.	**Directions:** Answer _____ of the questions below.
Who is it about?	**Who is it about?**
What happened?	**What happened?**
When did it happen?	**When did it happen?**
Where is the story taking place?	**Where is the story taking place?**
Why did it happen?	**Why did it happen?**
How did the character feel?	**How did the character feel?**

Millionaire Game

LIFELINE: *Ask the Audience*

A) Totally Understand It   **C**) Confused

B) Think I Get It   **D**) Totally Lost

Supervisor

Supervisor

Supervisor

Text Message Summary

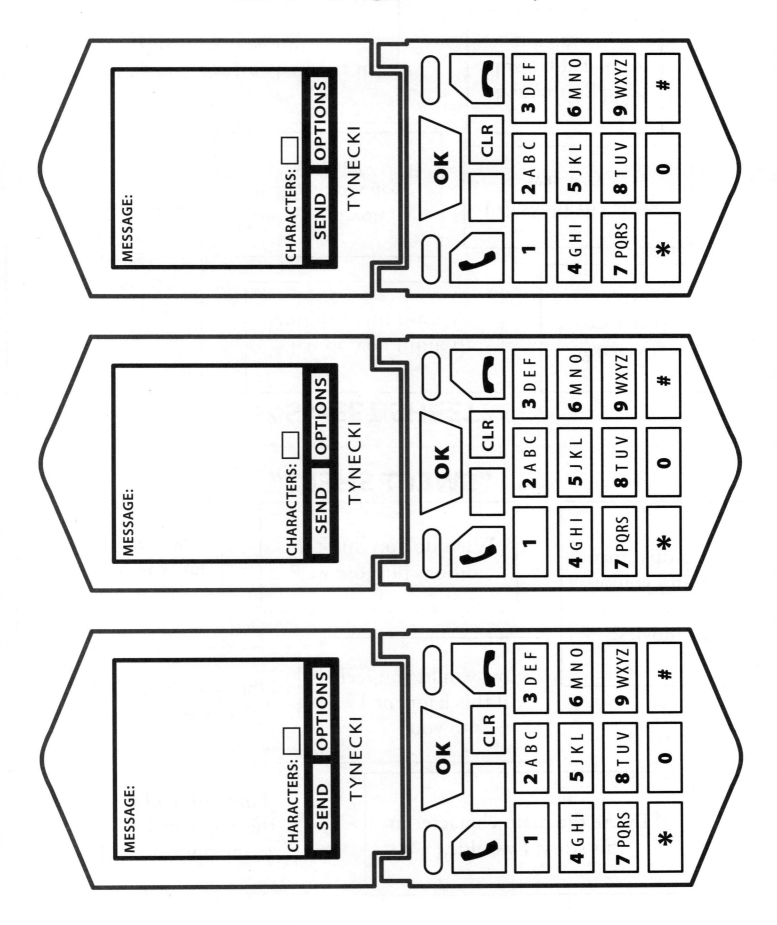

"SWEET SHEET"

Something like
this happened to
me once…

If I were the main character in
this story, I would…

I thought the author
was very…

How would you feel
if this happened
to you?

What was your
favorite part of the
story?

What do you think the
author's purpose was?

Does this story
remind you of
any other stories
or movies?

FOLD

"SWEET SHEET"

Does this story
remind you of
any other stories
or movies?

What do you think the
author's purpose was?

What was your
favorite part of the
story?

How would you feel
if this happened
to you?

I thought the author
was very…

If I were the main character in
this story, I would…

Something like
this happened to
me once…

"SWEET SHEET"

Would you recommend this book to anyone else? If so, to whom?

I thought it was kind of crazy when…

I would rewrite this story so that…

My favorite part, so far, was…

Do you think it is a believable story so far?

I was a bit confused when…

What actor do you think would play the main character in a movie?

FOLD

"SWEET SHEET"

What actor do you think would play the main character in a movie?

I was a bit confused when…

Do you think it is a believable story so far?

My favorite part, so far, was…

I would rewrite this story so that…

I thought it was kind of crazy when…

Would you recommend this book to anyone else? If so, to whom?

Lightbulb Moments

Colorful Speech

Directions: Place a colored cube under each word in the sentence.
Use the key below. Then connect the cubes to show the sentence.

☐ Blue = Noun
☐ Red = Verb
☐ Brown = Pronoun
☐ Yellow = Preposition
☐ Orange = Adverb
☐ Green = Adjective
☐ Black = Article

1. The ice cream dripped on the floor.

2. Chocolate is my favorite candy.

3. The sky grew cloudy last night.

4. I finished my homework!

Stepping Stones Variation

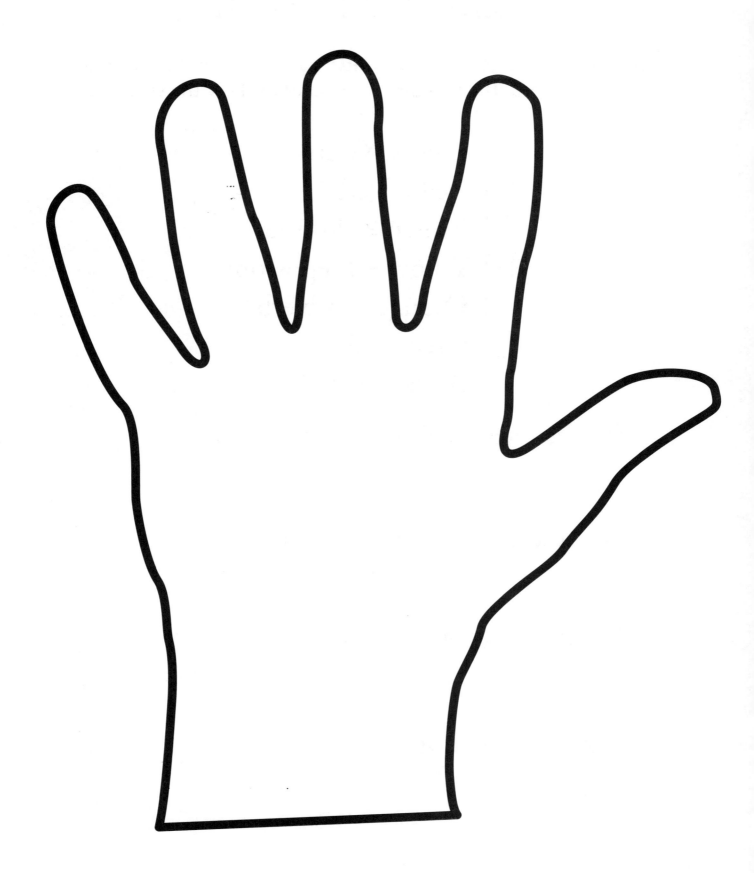

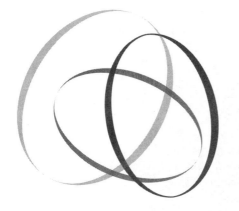

Index

Note: Page numbers in **boldface** indicate reproducibles.